# Happily Ever After

## IS A CHOICE

A Woman's Transformational Guide
to Finding True Love

MARIA MUGICA

eBook ISBN: 978-1-965761-43-4
Paperback ISBN: 978-1-965761-44-1
Hardcover ISBN: 978-1-965761-46-5
Ingram Spark ISBN: 978-1-965761-45-8
Library of Congress Control Number: 2025906531

Editor: Megan McConnell
Cover Design: Angela Ayala
Interior Design: Marigold2K
Author Photos: https://www.vanvo.photography/
Publisher: Spotlight Publishing House –
https://spotlightpublishinghouse.com

# Happily Ever After

## IS A CHOICE

A Woman's Transformational Guide
to Finding True Love

## MARIA MUGICA

SPOTLIGHT
PUBLISHING HOUSE

Goodyear, Arizona

# *Endorsements*

"I believe with all my heart that *Happily Ever After is a Choice* will be a game-changer for women who have struggled to find a meaningful, loving relationship. It is a beautifully crafted guide that offers both inspiration and practical tools to transform your love life. I thoroughly enjoyed reading it and was moved by Maria's courage and honesty. Her insights are spot-on, and her guidance is precisely what so many women need."

**—Jaki Sabourin**
Author of Engaged at Any Age: A Proven Path to Love Over 40

"If you've given up on love, read this book! You'll feel inspired and refreshed. Maria has created a down-to-earth guide; this book is the lantern to light your way."

**— Suzanne Adams**
Bestselling Author of Girl Awakened and Quantum Vibes

"Maria Mugica is sharing not just her stories in *Happily Ever After is a Choice*, but her wisdom, and a way to make this work for anyone looking for that happily ever after for themselves. Following her guidance, you can have that wonderful life, too! Having witnessed Maria's journey and knowing her at both professional and personal levels, I can be the first to testify to the value that is contained within the pages of this incredible book!"

**— Lin Yuan-Su**
Success Coach, Author and Speaker, Founder of Enlightened Success Institute

"*Happily Ever After is a Choice* is a beautifully crafted, deeply personal, and transformational guide to love, healing, and self-discovery. Maria Mugica weaves together her own heartfelt journey with practical wisdom, soulful reflections, and actionable steps to help women release past wounds and open their hearts to the love they truly deserve. Her vulnerability and insight make this book a powerful companion for any woman seeking to align with the energy of true love. This isn't just a book about finding a partner—it's a sacred invitation to embrace yourself fully, walk with faith, and create a love story that resonates with your soul. A must-read for anyone ready to step into the highest vision of love!"

**— Rev. Cynthia Ambriz**
Spiritual Therapist & Coach, Author of Life Finds a Way: A Journey of Healing and Return to Wholeness

"Have you ever read a book that inspires hope, warms your heart and blows you away with the author's authenticity and passion? A true love story filled with the ability to transform the reader's life, Happily Ever After is a Choice is the "just right" book for women who have given up on finding "The One" yet are willing to give love one more chance.

Maria Mugica's journey is a powerful testament to the transformational power of self-love, God's love, faith, and devotion. Through her struggles and pain, she refused to give up. She was determined to remove the barriers keeping love at bay.

Through deep inner work, she not only manifested her husband as a first- time bride after the age of 50 but also became a guiding light for other women on their paths to love.

In *Happily Ever After is a Choice: A Woman's Transformational Guide to Finding True Love*, Maria shares her personal story with remarkable vulnerability and wisdom. Her journey, combined with inspirational insights, humor, journal prompts, and practical steps, make this book an invaluable guide for any woman seeking lasting love.

I wholeheartedly believe this book will be a game-changer. Maria's wisdom, honesty, and step-by-step guidance will empower you to open your heart, clear the blocks to love, and create the relationship you desire."
— **Ayanna Mojica**
Founder, Feminine Wealth Brand Legacy

# Dedication

To my husband Eric,
there is no one else I would rather be here with than you.

# Table of Contents

## SECTION SEVEN

# Foreword

When Maria Mugica joined my year-long coaching program, she was determined to remove the blocks that were keeping love at a distance and manifest a husband. With a strong foundation in personal development, Maria embraced the self-mastery processes I taught with devotion and quickly became a leader within our community. Her empathy and supportive nature made her a natural coach, and she soon started helping other women navigate their journeys. Her dedication to the work and her gentle spirit were invaluable at our live events, where she played an essential role.

Maria's commitment to breaking down her barriers to love led her to meet and marry a wonderful husband. Her journey is a shining example of what is possible when you commit to growth, self-love, and the courage to choose love every day.

In *Happily Ever After is a Choice: A Woman's Transformational Guide to Finding True Love*, Maria bravely shares her personal story with such vulnerability that it touched my heart deeply. Her willingness to be open about her own experiences is one of her greatest strengths—it is the very quality that most men seek in a partner. This book is filled with inspirational quotes that align perfectly with each lesson she teaches, along with personal anecdotes and stories from her journey to finding love. She does not stop there—Maria provides a practical, step-by-step process with journal prompts and actionable practices that will help you make the necessary changes to find and sustain a loving relationship.

I believe with all my heart that this book will be a game-changer for women who have struggled to find a meaningful, loving relationship. It is a beautifully crafted guide that offers both inspiration and practical tools to transform your love life. I thoroughly enjoyed reading it and was moved by Maria's courage and honesty. Her insights are spot-on, and her guidance is precisely what so many women need.

I do not doubt that *Happily Ever After is a Choice* will help you create the love story you have always dreamed of. Trust in Maria's wisdom, follow her guidance, and watch your life transform.

With love and confidence in your journey,

Jaki Sabourin
Author of *Engaged at Any Age: A Proven Path to Love Over 40*

# Preface

Welcome to your journey to love with me at your side. I am honored you would choose this book, or perhaps it chose you. The things I did to prepare for my beloved husband and the way we met have inspired many women, which inspired me to create a guide for those who wish for the same. I have included practices that I used first to prepare myself and then prepare for him to enter my life and eventually become a first-time bride at fifty-two.

My road to love was arduous, wrought with much heartache and disappointment. Many times, I had given up hope and made peace with being a fabulous single woman. I would focus on my career and keep men at bay. However, the voice within, no matter how soft, would remind me of my longing and desire to be in a loving relationship. That seemed like such a tall order since I had yet to experience or even witness such a thing.

Like most girls, I was raised on fairy tales that ended with the following: *And they lived happily ever after.* In my teen years, the rom-coms had the nerdy girl end up with the cool boy. I longed to meet my man and have a fairy-tale romance. However, I was not attracting what I longed for.

After many rounds of unhealthy relationships, I took a long break from dating. Even though a part of me had given up on love, the little voice inside said she did not want to give up. However, I was not sure how to do it in a way that did not end up with me crying on the bathroom floor. So, without a road map and only a dream, I took my first steps. The pages that follow contain many of the steps I took, nuggets of wisdom from the teachers I studied, and the practices that I embodied.

When I would share about my journey to love and the synchronistic way my husband and I met, most people said, you should write a book. So, I did. A layoff from a sixteen-year career freed me up to fulfill a dream of walking 500 miles across Spain on the Camino de Santiago. There, I carried a prayer in my backpack to meet my beloved. Upon my return, I volunteered to help a captain friend deliver a boat along the California Coast. The weather conditions were extreme and unpleasant. Who would ever expect I was about to meet my beloved? Certainly not me!

I am a very spiritual person. I use many terms for my co-creator and higher power. In *Happily Ever After is a Choice: A Woman's Transformational Guide to Finding True Love,* you may see me use the names God, the Universe, and Infinite Intelligence to describe a higher power. We are not alone in building our dreams. There is a Power breathing us. As Paolo Coelho writes in his spiritual novel *The Alchemist, "When you want something, all the universe conspires in helping you achieve it."*

In *Happily Ever After is a Choice*, I use the name Ginnie to represent a compilation of female friends and clients whose relevant stories I use as examples to highlight specific points. I chose this name because a wonderful woman named Ginnie was my mentor as a teen, seeing the adventure and magic in me before I could see it in myself.

*Happily Ever After is a Choice* is written so you may read it sequentially, cover to cover, or flip it open to a page for inspiration and a focus for the day.

Throughout the book, I share many excellent resources that were indispensable on my journey to love. The "Reference & Resource" section at the end of the book lists all of them.

If a part of you has given up on love, I want you to know that if true love can happen for me, even though I, too, had given up, it is also possible for you. Let me be your guide. May your dream of finding your true love be realized. Yet, your true gift can be the woman you become in the process. This is the really juicy stuff!

Wishing you a love-filled adventure,

"Mrs." Maria Mugica-German

# Acknowledgments

I want to thank all those teachers, coaches, and mentors who helped me along my journey to love so that I finally became the woman who could attract and sustain a healthy, loving relationship.

So much of my inner foundational work came because of an early spiritual teacher, Vajra, who helped me heal multiple lifetimes and nursed me back to wholeness after I allowed unhealthy relationships to debilitate me. When she attempted to show me what a healthy partnership could look like, I balked because it seemed so boring. Thankfully, I got here. A healthy relationship is not boring at all; it is steady.

An event that launched my first steps toward love was a virtual Soulmate Summit held by Arielle Ford and Claire Zammit. I purchased the workbook and CDs, which I listened to for hours upon hours while I drove the territory I covered for my work from Los Angeles to San Diego. It ingrained a new operating system and understanding of myself and men.

I am so grateful for Alison Armstrong's teachings. She is the most amazing teacher about men. Her work helped me see men in a new way, with such love and appreciation. I learned their language and truly discovered the gift they are in my life. I was forever transformed, and I took a vow never to castrate a man with my words again.

Jackie Sabourin was my love coach the year I met Eric. She helped me navigate this new world of love and relationships while the other ladies in her Engaged at Any Age community cheered me on.

To my rag-tag team of Camino companions, Carla, Silvio, Guillaume, and Martin, who I spent hours upon hours and days upon days walking beside. Thank you for the laughter, adventure, and support and for accepting me as I am. I am grateful for the synchronistic ways our separate journeys collided into a shared path. Our deep conversations, balanced with jokes and laughter, matched the ever-changing terrain.

Many thanks to Junie Swadron, my writing coach and accountability partner, who spent months helping me write my book and process some of the pieces from my past that still needed attention and healing.

To Mary Morrisey and the Brave Thinking Institute faculty, who taught me the principles and discipline for manifesting the life of my dreams. The tools I learned helped me turn the dream of this book into a physical reality.

To Ayanna Mojica, who holds the codes to female empowerment, sacred sexuality, and feminine wealth. Her generosity and grace support all who seek her guidance.

Thanks to my parents, Margaret and Victor Mugica. They provided a safe, loving home, a strong community, strong values, and a great education. They have always supported my dreams, even if they did not quite understand them, and have given me a solid foundation so that when I was ready, I could fly.

And to my husband, Eric, the answer to my prayers. Thank you for being you.

# Introduction

Have you given up on love? There was a time when I gave up, too. Like many little girls, I was raised on fairy tales like Snow White and Cinderella. As a teen, I watched romantic films that ranged from *Roman Holiday* to *Sixteen Candles*. I was a closet hopeless romantic because I felt embarrassed to admit to liking any boy.

I so desired to meet my prince and live happily ever after. I spent decades making poor choices that resulted in endless disappointment and broken hearts. It was exhausting. I could not trust myself to make a good choice in relation to men. So, I gave up, focused on my career, and decided that being single was far easier and less of a hassle. Yet, the longing to meet my beloved would weave its way back into my consciousness. Eventually, I could no longer ignore it. Thus began my journey to love.

In this book, I guide you in preparing for and manifesting the love of your life. I blend inspiring quotes about love and manifestation with stories from my personal journey, sharing solutions to the challenges I faced along the way. I also offer insights I gained from leading relationship experts and create a space for you, the reader, to engage in reflection through journal prompts, inspired actions, and mindfulness practices.

As a first-time bride at the age of fifty-two, I am proof that it is never too late to find true love. I spent years studying men and my relationship with them. I attended events with some of the top relationship experts and participated in every possible webinar, summit, and podcast about love. During a 500-mile walking pilgrimage across Spain on the Camino De Santiago, I carried a prayer in my backpack to meet my beloved. A month after returning from my journey, I met my now-husband on a boat in San Francisco Bay. The circumstances were wild and made for a great story, regardless of whether we ended up together or not.

The good news is that we did end up together! When I shared the story of how we met, people, especially women, would tell me that I had to write a book. So, here it is! I am passionate about connecting with and inspiring women over forty who have given up on love. I love sharing my story of overcoming decades of disappointment and broken hearts to tell my happily ever after story. I know that if true love can happen for me, it can happen for you, too.

My intention in writing this book and sharing my story is to inspire women —you— not to give up on your dream of true love. I hope that the quotes throughout the book open you up to a deeper truth and understanding of what is possible. May my personal journey and experiences help you see that you are not alone. If it is your dream to meet and marry the love of your life, it can happen for you, too.

In "Section One, Preparing Yourself for Love," you will assess your progress in various areas of your life. This step helps you determine how much time and commitment you are willing to invest in the process. It will also help you feel a sense of joyful anticipation as you set your intention to prepare for your beloved.

In order to make room for something new, you need to make space for it. That includes your interior self as well. I help you review your past relationships to see if any emotional spaces need clearing through forgiveness. Then, I show you how to install new patterns and thoughts. I provide simple yet powerful practices to help you move any stuck energies to make room for something beautiful and new.

# INTRODUCTION

Preparing for your man can be so much fun. I share ways that music, prayers, and art can enhance your physical and energetic space. I encourage you to open your mind to new experiences by expanding your comfort zone and asking for help from the people around you. You will be reminded of the practice of gratitude during your love journey and beyond.

Next, it is time to set your intention and gain clarity on what you truly desire. I spent several years working with Mary Morrissey and the Brave Thinking Institute to master the principles of manifestation. I share some of these principles and help you to envision and write down your deepest desires for love as part of a process to create the life of your dreams.

In "Section Five: Pilgrimage, Prayer, and Spanish Rice," I share my 500-mile pilgrimage on the Camino de Santiago with a prayer in my backpack to meet my beloved. Then, join my adventure from San Francisco down the coast of California, where I first met my now husband, Eric. The wild seas tossed us around, and I became extremely seasick, yet despite this, Eric and I bonded during this adrenaline-pumping experience. But it was my family recipe for Spanish Rice that kept us in touch afterward.

Getting to the church on time is just the beginning. Then, your happily ever after is a choice you make daily. Our relationships are a wonderful reflection of our beauty and opportunities for growth. With everything I share in *Happily Ever After is a Choice,* you can rewrite your "love story" and create the life of your dreams.

If you have given up on love, this book will inspire you to change your mindset. The practices in the book are meant to support you in self-reflection and inspired action. Your man already exists. Now, you can work on becoming a vibrational match to the perfect person for you. Then, you, too, can have the best how-we-met story to share with friends and family.

While I was on a call with the woman who would become my love coach the year I met Eric, something deep within me rose up to express, *"I just don't want to live another year without him!"* I did not know who *he* was, but the longing was so intense that it pushed me to invest in the support of a coach. I urge you not to wait another minute if your greatest desire is to be with the love of your life. This book is the best investment you can make to set you on the path to meeting your man.

Know that I am cheering for you, and I can't wait to hear all about your love story!

# Section One

## PREPARING YOURSELF FOR LOVE

*"If you prepare yourself at every point as well as you can, with whatever means you may have, however meager they may seem, you will be able to grasp opportunity for broader experience when it appears. Without preparation you cannot do it."*

~Eleanore Roosevelt

# Preparing For True Love

*"We are Physical, Mental, and Spiritual beings. If you don't deal with ALL OF LIFE, you're not going to get all that life has to offer."*
~ Zig Ziglar

Suppose your love life has had its ups and downs, and being in a long-term, healthy, loving relationship is more foreign than natural. In that case, you must consider committing as much time and energy to the endeavor of finding true love as a runner prepares for a marathon or a bride prepares for her wedding.

Getting physically, mentally, spiritually, and emotionally prepared for the journey will benefit you greatly. The journey is not just about the result but also about the woman you are becoming in the process.

It is so important to feel at home in your skin. I know many women tell themselves that as soon as they lose weight, they will get out there and date. This is a great delay tactic. It allows us to think that we are making progress, yet it prevents us from taking action in the direction of our dream of finding love.

I have simple weekly routines that keep me physically moving and my body feeling good. I walk outdoors most days and commit to a short Yoga or Pilates practice three to five times a week with some of my favorite teachers on the internet. If you are a woman who does not have a regular workout practice, find something you love, such as riding a bike or taking a dance class. Start small and work your way up. Just keep moving!

When it comes to food and eating, I have had my ups and downs, been on diets, and only sometimes at my optimal weight. Currently, my focus is on the quality of my food and smaller meals.

I prefer whole foods, lots of vegetables, minimal processing, minimal meat, and organic foods whenever possible. A commitment to your health and well-being is part of a self-care practice. Small steps can lead to significant changes over time. Do it lovingly.

My experience with men is that they are attracted not only to a woman's physical aspects but also to her energy and life force. Good men love strong, confident women who are authentic and full of life. Know that you are worthy of love regardless of whether or not you are at your ideal weight.

Mental preparation for love is about setting your intentions and committing to the journey. Decide that you want to meet your beloved and are willing to do what it takes to become the woman you need to be to attract a wonderful partner. Engaging in the practices in this book will help you become clear about who you are, what you want, and what deserves your loving attention.

Relying on the support of a Higher Being to co-create with you during this process is an essential spiritual practice. You are not alone in this endeavor. Adding meditation, mindfulness, and prayer to help achieve your dream makes the journey flow even more. Universal Intelligence is ready to bring our desires to fruition when we are a vibrational match. I share more about this in "Section Four: Crafting Your Vision."

Emotional preparation involves organizing your internal space. If you need more in-depth insights and guidance, consider reaching out to a coach or therapist. Sometimes, it might be wise to pause dating and take time to reflect on your inner self, your patterns, and your beliefs before moving forward. Only you can determine the best path. This book provides practices that can assist you in navigating this part of your journey.

My friend Ginnie spent several years on her couch after a painful divorce. She is an attractive woman and had no trouble dating during this time; however, the relationships did not work out, leaving her feeling sad, lonely, and disappointed time and again. Ginnie decided she needed a break from dating and enrolled in a coaching program. She worked to become a certified coach while also focusing on her personal growth throughout the year-long program. She took a deep dive into herself, addressing the parts that needed healing. She learned tools to help her assess her triggers and discover healthy ways to process her emotions.

When she finally felt ready to meet her man, she had professional photos taken, relaunched her dating profile, and met the man who would become her husband within a month of returning to the dating scene.

# What Would You Do for Love?

---

*"There is one elementary truth...*
*that the moment one definitely commits oneself,*
*then providence moves too."*
~ William Hutchinson Murray

After realizing and admitting to yourself and others that you genuinely desire to meet the love of your life, one of the most essential steps is committing to doing what it takes to become the person you need to be to meet your true love.

The quote above from Scottish explorer W.H. Murray reminds us that when we fully commit to something, universal law steps in. He goes on to say, *"A whole stream of events issues from the decision, raising in one's favor all manner of unforeseen incidents, meetings, and material assistance..."*

The year I met my now-husband, Eric, I had been laid off from my sixteen-year career. Even during this major life event, I still desired to meet my beloved. Although I had been considering a love coach to keep me inspired and on track, I was hesitant to sign up because I felt financially unstable without a job.

However, my commitment to finding my love partner was so strong that I took a deep breath, knowing in my heart it was the right

7

decision and chose to work with someone. There were other things I was willing to let go of, but not this. I was dedicated to finding my beloved. I am so happy I trusted myself. The guidance and support I received from my coach and her program kept me accountable for taking the steps that ultimately led me to Eric. I never imagined that taking the leap and signing a one-year contract when I did not have a steady paycheck would lead me to my desired results.

Are you ready to commit to the process of meeting your beloved? It does require an investment of time and money to prepare. Are you willing to invest in that which is your greatest longing and desire—to meet your beloved?

Where do you invest your time now? Many of us spend a minimum of forty hours a week working to make a living. Do you binge-watch streaming shows? Do you get caught down the rabbit hole of scrolling through social media? There is usually more time in our lives than we realize to commit to our heart's desire. Some of the things you could commit time to are reading books like this and doing the practices, attending workshops or programs related to love and relationships. Then, take time to be on dating sites, create your profile, set up times to communicate with men, and go on dates.

Where do you invest your money now? If you look at your credit card statements, you will see where the majority of your expendable cash goes. Is it daily morning lattes, new clothes, dinners out, or delivered? Many of us have invested thousands of dollars in college or training programs to find good jobs. It is culturally accepted to invest a significant amount of money in education.

Are you willing to make a financial investment for a successful love life? It could involve working with a dating coach or therapist. You may invest in a higher pay level of a dating site, pay for professional photos, purchase a new dating wardrobe, or commit to a year-long program to prep for love.

## SECTION ONE: PREPARING YOURSELF FOR LOVE

Looking back, I see that I spent several years preparing myself for love. I invested thousands of dollars in books, summits, workshops, training guides, and, eventually, a love coach. The rewards were multiple. Not only did I finally meet my man, who became my husband, but it is also who I became in the process, and that is such a wonderful gift.

# Self-Care
## On the Road to Love

———❤———

*"So mend, restore, redress—*
*when fishermen can't go to sea, they repair their nets."*
~ Ralph Blum The Book of Runes

I have always loved this quote from Ralph Blum's book, *The Book of Runes*. I find it comforting because it reminds me that it is ok to take time out from a project or a busy life. You can still use that time creatively. Sometimes, the journey to love can feel like it is taking forever. I would start each year ready to meet my man. Then, I would have a few disappointing dates that made me want to give up. It can feel like a setback and as though it is never going to happen. It is ok to take some time to rest, reevaluate, and *"repair your nets."* Be kind to yourself and allow yourself a little break. However, even your time-out can be used to prepare for your beloved.

Many times, I wanted to give up on finding love. In my low points, I believed that the dream of a healthy, loving partnership was not in the cards for me. When I needed a break from dating, I would get creative and start preparing my home for his arrival. I would clean out my closets and drawers to make space for something new. I made sure that I kept what I decided was his side of the bed and nightstand clean and placed items that I thought he might use. I let go of my chipped and broken dish set and purchased a new one, along with candles, in anticipation of his arrival and our romantic dinners.

11

I would listen to podcasts and webinars from experts on men, love, relationships, and dating to improve my knowledge and gain inner awareness of my habits and patterns that no longer served me in my quest for love. Loving yourself, maintaining high energy and vibration, and keeping your home physically and energetically clear are all in service to your vision.

When you need a time-out from actively dating, what are some fun ways you can prepare yourself, your home, or your things to make room for your beloved?

The most important self-care practice is learning to love and accept yourself 100% as you are. Getting rest, unplugging from social media and the internet, practicing yoga, meditating, getting bodywork, and taking walks in nature are some of the ways I take care of myself.

# Making Space for Love

―♥―

*"First best is falling in love.*
*Second best is being in love.*
*Least best is falling out of love.*
*But any of it is better than never having been in love."*
~ Maya Angelou

As I considered making space for love, I had fun exploring the art of Feng Shui. I do not pretend to be a Feng Shui expert, but I used guidance from books like *Move Your Stuff, Change Your Life: How to Use Feng Shui to Get Love, Money, Respect, and Happiness by* Karen Rauch Carter and by looking online. In the simplest terms, it is the art of placement in relation to the flow of energy. It is believed that there are areas of your home or bedroom that are the best places for attracting more love into your life. While I cannot prove its validity, I had fun decorating, de-cluttering, and making space for love.

I was not someone who had a lot of pink or red in my wardrobe or among my things, but I was guided to add more of these colors to my love corner. Even before my sweetheart showed up in my life, I made sure I had two matching nightstands on either side of my queen-sized bed. I picked his side and added a few books and items I thought he might enjoy. I emptied a drawer and shelf in the bathroom for him. I made room in my closet for his clothes.

The first weekend Eric stayed with me, he needed to buy a razor and shaving cream. Up until then, he had yet to leave anything at my place. When he was packing his things to head out on Sunday back to work, I asked him if he was taking his razor and shaving cream. He replied, *"Oh, I will just leave it here."* Lo and behold, he already had an empty shelf waiting for him. And he left his toothbrush, too.

I remember hearing love expert Arielle Ford talk about how many single women have single women in their artwork. When I looked around my apartment, I noticed I was 100% guilty of that. As a matter of fact, I had a card displayed of a nude woman pensively sitting at the base of a beautiful tree. I could look further into the meaning for me, but suffice it to say, once I became aware of my taste in art, I removed her and started to add loving couples. I went online and ordered stacks of cards with images of couples—lovers kissing on a Parisian street, couples holding hands, and dancing. I switched out my single-lady artwork and displayed these new images around my home. Once I figured out the recommended love corner in my bedroom, I set up an altar with love poems, prayers, candles, and loving images.

De-cluttering feels good to me and, at the very least, feels natural around springtime. I have come to realize that to make room for something new, whether new items or a new man, you need to let go of the past, physically and metaphorically.

I encourage you to let go of old letters, pictures, and memorabilia from past lovers. I supported my friend Ginnie with a bonfire at the beach as she burned her old wedding photos a decade-plus after her divorce. It opened a doorway for someone new. She is now in a new relationship and happily engaged.

# If You See Something You Love, Claim It!

———◆———

*"You get what you focus on, so focus on what you want."*
~ Author Unknown

I know that when I was single and longing for a relationship, I would sometimes feel so sad and lonely and even jealous when I saw couples walking around holding hands and being in love. Somewhere along the journey, I learned that it was better to be in appreciation of what I witnessed and turn it towards me in a positive way. I retrained myself and my neural pathways by focusing on the positive. When I saw a couple in love being affectionate, I would say, *"Oh, I like that!"* or *"I'm next!"* When I started to focus on and notice men caring for women in a way that I desired in my own life, I would say, *"Hey God, I would love a man like that in my life."*

The way I think of neural pathways is like when you see a well-worn path on a hiking trail. When many walkers, hikers, and cyclists use the same trail over and over, it is clear to see and easier to follow than forging a new path. So, when you are trying to create a new habit, it is like going off the trail. If you are the only one walking it, you will not see the new trail unless you do it day after day. Then, the new path becomes more visible and easier and natural to walk. So, too, new habits or thoughts need to be practiced on a daily basis to make an in-road in your life and actions.

When Eric and I first met on a three-day journey at sea, I was unaware that he would be *the one*. I noticed all the gestures he made that I truly appreciated. At that time, I was learning to identify what I liked and claim it for myself. Not only did Eric offer to hold my hair when I was losing my cookies over the side of the boat, but he also kept an eye on me. He prepared my dinner when I was still feeling awful. The sleeping berth we shared was leaking, and all our sleeping gear got wet. Finally, when it warmed up, and the sun came out, he pulled everything to the top of the boat to dry, then folded it all and brought it back down to the berth. I was so amazed by his generosity in these small acts of care. He did so many sweet and helpful things that I found myself creating a checklist, letting God know I liked this and wanted a man who would treat me this way.

He was a fantastic sailing partner. He was very kind and patient with me even though he got stuck with the least seasoned sailor. Then, low and behold, my feelings started to change towards him, and he fulfilled so much more of my checklist.

I love observing a man walking with his woman across the street and witnessing when he puts his hand at the base of her back as they cross. I see it as an act of protection and care. Now, when Eric does that with me, I am still amazed that I manifested it in my own life. It delights me to observe the ways men show love. It could be taking his wife's car in for an oil change. It could be holding the car door open and closing it for his sweetheart. I loved discovering that many men perform acts of service for the people that they love and care for. We women just need to take notice.

In the first year of our courtship, Eric made a point of changing the bulb in my burned-out headlight and washing the inside of my car windows so I could see out of them safely. This is a way that Eric shows his love for me through acts of service for my overall safety. I love acknowledging how much his kind acts mean to me. I do not want him ever to think I take them for granted. Here's a secret, ladies: Men LOVE being thanked for their acts of support. Don't we all?

# Love Practices

## Section One

# *Journal Reflection*

Purchase a beautiful LOVE journal for your LOVE Journey.

What steps are you willing to take this week to further your commitment to finding your ideal partner?

Where are you in the love journey process mentally, physically, emotionally, and financially?

Write out all the attributes you love about yourself. Reread it three times a day or as needed.

# *Inspired Action*

With fresh eyes, observe what kind of art you have in your home, especially your bedroom.

Have fun adding colorful décor and artwork depicting loving couples around your home.

Create a love corner and spend time reading love poems by candlelight.

Notice what you are noticing. Do you feel sad or angry when you see loving couples displaying affection? Perhaps it is time to start saying, *"I'm next!"*

Spend a week noticing when men do good things and perform noble actions. This will start to train you to look for the good and expect positive experiences with men.

## Mindfulness/Meditation

Though Eric and I have different tastes when it comes to what we read, one day, he picked up a book from my collection called *Love Yourself Like Your Life Depends On It* by Kamal Ravikant. It is an easy read with a profound message that Eric took to heart and put into practice. The author, in a time of great sorrow and despair, made a vow to himself that changed the trajectory of his life. He vowed to truly and deeply love himself each moment he is consciously able to make that decision. You, too, can decide to love yourself as if your life depends on it. Any time you are in need of this, place your hand on your heart, breathe fully yet gently, and repeat out loud or to yourself, *"I love myself."*

# Section Two

## HEALING YOUR LOVE WOUNDS

Last night as I was sleeping,
I dreamt—marvelous error!—that
I had a beehive
here inside my heart.
And the golden bees
were making white combs
and sweet honey
from my old failures.

~ Antonio Machado
"Last Night As I Lay Sleeping"

# All Men Are...

———♥———

*"Some women turn frogs into princes.*
*But that takes a queen, not a princess—or a shrew.*
*Like most women, you, my dear, turn princes into frogs!"*
~ Alison A. Armstrong

I was scrolling on a popular communication platform when I came across a post from a friend I had not seen in quite a while. She declared that dating gave her digestive issues. Then, a series of posts from other women who agreed followed. There were classic comments like *"Online dating is exhausting"* and *"Men are so disappointing, cheap, play games, are unreliable, and do not really want a relationship."* A brave man chimed in, stating he stopped dating because, in his experience, all women thought that way. While those women's comments and beliefs may have some truth based on their experiences, they create a wall to what they truly desire: a loving relationship.

As a happily married woman and a recovered man-basher, I refrained from telling the ladies on that post that if they did not change their thoughts and beliefs, they would never meet a good man. Instead, I have saved that message for those of you reading this book. If you change your negative thoughts about men and dating, you will alter the trajectory of your dating life and become available to meet the man of your dreams.

Growing up, I learned from the women around me, in less-than-perfect marriages, as well as popular culture, that men can be so disappointing because they do not listen and are emotionally unavailable. If you keep attracting men who seem to be the opposite of what you hoped for, it is crucial to spend some time uncovering your beliefs about men in general. Some are likely unconscious, so you may need time to explore.

Some common ones are:

- All the good men are taken
- You cannot count on a man
- They never follow through
- Just when I get close, they take off
- They only want one thing
- They do not listen or get me

Your experiences of how men do or do not show up for you can be a clue to some of your unconscious beliefs about men. For example, I attracted men who left shortly after they arrived. There was a part of me that feared intimacy and getting too close because I did not want to be invested if they left me, and I was then left with an even bigger broken heart. Because of this unconscious belief at the time, I attracted and repelled men repeatedly. As the quote above claims, I may have turned some princes into frogs.

Alison Armstrong, author, educator, and creator of the widely acclaimed *Understanding Men* and *Understanding Women* transformational online series, has done fantastic work helping men and women better understand and communicate with each other. After exposure to her work and the goodness of men, my paradigm was turned upside down. I now see men's generosity and innate desire to care for and support women. When we are at our best, they want to be in our presence and support our endeavors.

Ginnie did not feel ready to date after her divorce. It was difficult for her to believe she could trust any man again. I suggested she begin practicing getting to know men in situations where she did not have to invest a lot of emotional energy in the relationship. So, she started observing and interacting with the men she worked with in a new way. She would ask them how their day was going, then remain silent and listen to their reply. By staying quiet and attentive, she noticed how they sometimes revealed more about their day and life in general.

Over time, she became aware that some male colleagues gravitated to her calm, feminine presence. They trusted her and the positive rapport that was built. She started to trust herself in relation to them as well. Confidence and discernment returned to her, and eventually, she felt ready to put herself out there and start dating.

# How to Get Over
## Your Ex-Lovers

———❤———

*"My weaknesses have always been food and men—in that order."*
~ Dolly Parton

This area of life can be challenging, so I am injecting some humor through the quote above. In the past, I was an expert at obsessing and suffering over old lovers and crushes. When I look back, it was like I had a crazy mind and was completely addicted to the person or, more accurately, the idea of him. I cannot believe how much I let myself suffer from pining.

In my youth, I was capable of the most intense crushes. I would obsess about the object of my affection day and night. My crushes could last for many years but never become anything more than a fantasy. As I matured and became involved with my partners sexually, the obsession intensified due to the bonding hormone, oxytocin, and the happy hormone, dopamine. I had a pattern of attracting and being attracted to men where there was an overpowering draw and intense connection that ultimately could not be sustained. They often were gone as quickly as they arrived. The intense highs and lows were chaotic. When they left, they usually disappeared entirely from my life. The feelings of loss were devastating and sometimes took me years to overcome.

When the relationship ended, I felt empty and longed for them from sunup to sundown. They were often the first thing I thought of upon waking. With the object of my affection missing in action and no more dopamine hits, I felt like I was in withdrawal.

So, how do we navigate the loss and obsessive thoughts about an ex-partner? First, we need to honor any grief surrounding the loss. No matter if it was a long or short relationship, honor how you feel. Love and connection can happen quickly. We also attribute so many hopes and dreams to this one person and relationship. So, it appears that when they are gone, our hopes and dreams die with them.

As you are the highest authority of your life, look around and determine if there are things you can do to help sever unhealthy ties to a former partner. Unfollowing them from social media platforms is an excellent first step. You may need to block or delete their number. Are there letters to burn, photos to delete or rip up, clothes or gifts to return or give away?

In the past, I have written letters that were never sent but burned in a fire. If you cannot burn things, then rip them into many pieces and throw them out with the trash. Since I lived by the ocean for many years, I would sometimes find a suitable rock on the beach, hold it in my hands, and with intention fill it with all my hopes, dreams, anger, sadness, and grief. I would then set it on the sand and watch the tide take it out to sea.

We are energetic beings. When we are involved with one another, an energetic connection is formed. It may be helpful to use a process called cutting chords. In a private space, take three cleansing breaths. Then, get a sense of any energetic connections you may still feel towards a former partner. You may feel something in your heart area, or just above your belly button called the solar plexus, Chakra, or below the belly button where the Root and Sacral Chakra are. Even if you do not feel anything, you can use your imagination. See this person from your past about six to ten feet in front of you. Feel or imagine a cord or cords connecting you to this person. Then, with intention, call back your cord and your energy, see it disconnect from the other person, and come back to your energy field. If you find yourself unsure or struggling, call on your angels, guides, or your higher power to help you. You may do this process multiple times until it feels complete.

I learned this process from a spiritual practitioner who supported and guided me through it. It is a very powerful practice, especially when another person facilitates it. However, after learning it, I was able to use this technique on my own to help me release romantic partners from my past.

# How to Get Over Your Ex-Lovers:
## Installing New Thoughts

———❤———

*"God grant me the serenity to accept the things I cannot change,*
*the courage to change the things I can,*
*and the wisdom to know the difference."*
~ The Serenity Prayer

In the previous section, I shared ways to physically and ritualistically release your past relationships. While those are helpful practices, anyone who has been stuck on an ex-partner knows the repetitive and obsessive thoughts that you can experience.

Repetitive thoughts can involve reliving special or painful moments, fantasizing about ways to get them back, figuring out ways to have revenge, or having mental arguments. Any of these ways can keep you energetically tied to the person. If your goal is to break that pattern, I recommend that you set an intention to cease engaging in these unhealthy thoughts. Below is a practice to help you shift the pattern.

Process for Releasing Obsessive Thoughts, inspired by the Brave Thinking Institute:

- First, notice when you are in a mental loop of repetitive thinking about your ex or having a mental argument with them.
- Pause, inhale comfortably, then exhale like blowing through a straw. No force is necessary. Do this at least three times.
- Then, as you install a new thought, commit an affirmation or prayer to memory. The Serenity Prayer is a great example. The Ho'Oponopono Prayer is also helpful. It goes like this: I'm sorry, please forgive me, I love you, thank you.
- You may need to do this many times throughout the day if it is a fresh break-up.

As the years progressed, I became aware of how often I obsessed over my past relationships. Then, there came a moment when I realized I had what could be considered a love addiction. In my early years, I had no tools to support me, but I intuitively used long-distance walking and yoga to help me with repetitive thinking.

Knowing that I wanted to heal my addiction to unhealthy love relationships, I utilized spiritual practitioners, healers, and coaches to help me process, along with meditation and journaling. I participated in twelve-step programs to help gain awareness of my patterns, and I learned about magical thinking. When I felt powerless over my obsessive thoughts, I learned to give them over to my Higher Power.

All these things helped me move closer to a healthy mind and to heal the parts inside that needed healing. And miraculously to a place where I was finally able to attract a healthy, loving relationship with absolutely no addictive tendencies.

# How to Get Over Your Ex-Lovers:
## Forgiveness

---

*"I forgive you and set you free.*
*Your actions no longer have power over me.*
*I acknowledge that you are doing the best that you can,*
*and I honor you in your process of unfolding.*
*You are free, and I am free.*
*All is well between us.*
*Peace is the order of the day."*
~ Michael Bernard Beckwith

There are many forgiveness processes and techniques available; the one above is an excellent example. When I reflect on my experience of forgiveness, I realize that I am eclectic. I have used many different modalities and techniques to let go and forgive someone. It is an organic process for me, and I intuitively use what feels suitable for that particular person or incident.

Over the years, I have learned, and needed to be reminded, that forgiveness does not let the one who wronged me, or I believe wronged me, off the hook, but it helps release *me* from the hook. If we have been wronged or betrayed, forgiveness does not mean that it was okay, but it releases us from staying in the role of victim. We are freed because we no longer allow a person or situation to have power over us.

I invite you to walk through your memories and do a forgiveness process with any of your previous partners that come to mind. You may also want to spend some time forgiving your parents and caregivers. We are often attracting and attracted to a familiar dynamic that starts with the relationships we had as children.

Before getting to forgiveness, I often need to process the anger first. For the more intense ones, where I am seething with anger and having mental arguments about it, I have sought the support of a spiritual practitioner. It helps me to verbally get the issues off my chest with a neutral, compassionate listener who then offers me guidance and support as I move through my angst. If you do not have someone like that in your life, the Agape International Spiritual Center trains practitioners to hold space and pray with you. They have a directory, and it can be facilitated over the phone.

I have used writing to process my anger and resentment. I will write out all my thoughts and feelings without edits and with many expletives until I feel complete. Then, I will rip it up and toss it or burn it if I am able. This process can take many times and versions until it runs its course.

A *Course in Miracles* talks about a *"little willingness."* My interpretation of a little willingness is knowing that my small egoic mind wants to be right. In opening up to the Holy Spirit, I allow something greater than myself to move in and interpret the situation from a place of Love. Being able to see things differently helps make space for Spirit to move in and transform a situation.

Even when I do not feel like forgiving someone, I have prayed, "Dear God, I am so angry with XYZ right now that I do not feel like I can forgive them. Please help me so I can be free. I am willing to see them the way you see them," because I know it would be good for me to do so.

The Eternal Presence sees only our light and innocence. I am willing to be open and get a glimpse of that light so I may see them in their true radiance. This helps me be more open to letting go of my anger, judgment, or grudge towards that person.

I also use movement to help me process my anger. Walking to let off steam releases some of the energy and helps me regain my balance. You may consider dance, yoga, or martial arts to move the energy as well.

# The Benefits of Meeting
## a Divorced Man

---❤︎---

*"Don't try to be perfect; just be an excellent example of being human."*
~ Tony Robbins

While I had been longing for my beloved since my teen years, once I was in my forties, I was prepared to meet a man who had been married before and likely had children. Rather than focusing on how he looked and what he did for a living, my mantra was, *"I am loved, cherished, and adored."* I desired to be with a good man who was happy in his life and had his interests, along with some that dovetailed nicely with mine. More than anything, I wanted to be able to be in a healthy, loving relationship where I could be entirely myself. The good news is that my vision is now my reality, especially after I was able to love, cherish, and adore myself.

While Eric had been married before, he did not have children with his previous wife. Yet, he came with the sweetest dog named Sorrento. I know I got the best version of Eric. He chose to learn from his first marriage and do things differently and better. He also admits that being a dog owner taught him to be more responsible for another being.

When I have the opportunity, I ask men who are married to intelligent, confident women what they learned from their previous relationships that they are implementing now. The common theme I hear is that

37

they are trying to be better communicators and listeners. Many men are attracted to and love being with smart, successful women. Mature men, through life experience, know more about what they want and are willing to do to achieve their desires. I see them wanting to show up for their women in the best way they know how.

If you are reading this, your man is out there living his life and looking for you. He will be a compilation of all his life experiences, from how he was raised, to his past relationships, and current choices. We can be super specific about what we want our partner to be like, but humans are so complex, and each of us is unique. Just like you, your dream man will be dealing with life. Hold your vision for what you truly desire while keeping some space for the one the Universe has in store for you. You never know what treasures come in unexpected packages.

# Love Practices

## Section Two

# Journal Reflection

Spend time journaling about your beliefs about men and how they have or have not shown up for you. These are clues to your unconscious beliefs. We attract what we believe, whether we are aware of it or not.

In your journal, reflect on your feelings about a recent or past ex. If you still experience any grief or sadness, allow yourself to feel it without labeling it. Cry if that feels appropriate. Write down your emotions, and when the time feels right, tear up or burn the piece of paper.

# Inspired Action

Memorize or write an affirmation or prayer that will be easy to remember when you need to install a new thought pattern.

Take three easy breaths, exhaling like you are blowing through a straw. Then, either quietly or out loud, say your affirmation.

Repeat at least three times a day or as needed.

# Mindfulness/Meditation

Find some quiet time in the morning before your day begins or in the evening before you go to bed. Notice if there is someone, whether current or from your past, who comes to mind that you feel it is time to forgive. Place your hand on your heart and take some gentle, cleansing breaths. Visualize this person in your mind's eye if that feels comfortable.

After stating their name, recite the forgiveness quote by Michael Bernard Beckwith:

*"I forgive you and set you free.*
*Your actions no longer have power over me.*
*I acknowledge that you are doing the best that you can,*
*and I honor you in your process of unfolding.*
*You are free, and I am free.*
*All is well between us.*
*Peace is the order of the day."*

Then, pause and reflect on how it feels. Do you feel the need to repeat it a few more times, or do you feel complete at this moment? You can say it any time you sense the need.

# Section Three

## PREPARING FOR HIM

*"Fall in love with yourself, with life,
and then with whoever you want."*

~Frida Kahlo

# Devote Yourself to Something Greater Than You

---

*"The best way to find yourself is to lose yourself in the service of others."*
~ Gandhi

A couple of years prior to meeting Eric, I was in a relationship that I had hoped would turn into something more. However, it was not meant to be, and I felt very disappointed and sad. I spent mornings crying into my coffee.

Finally, I could not stand myself any longer, and I realized that I needed to get involved in something bigger than myself to get out of this rut. My predisposition was toward a spiritually centered community. I saw a new spiritual center advertised in the area. I went to a Sunday service shortly after and found some like-minded souls. Not only did I attend regular service, I got involved in the community. I volunteered for committees, signed up for classes, and connected over brunches and dinners with other members. This community helped me out of my self-indulgent rut of feeling sorry for myself. I have great friends and a support team to this day.

Around that time, I also joined a band that sang and performed sacred chants called Kirtan. We were invited to sing at spiritual centers, yoga studios, and fundraisers. It was a way for me to serve and give back with my time, talents, and voice.

Seva is Hindu for sacred or selfless service, a service that is performed without any hope of reciprocation, monetary benefits, or awards. I was not trying to get anything; I wanted to give. It was not my intention that it would get me a husband, but during that time, I was devoting myself to something greater than me. A spiritual teacher of mine acknowledged that my Seva was part of my offering to the Beloved for my beloved, who was on his way, whether I knew it or not.

After walking the 500-mile Camino de Santiago, a pilgrimage across Spain, I joined a local chapter of pilgrims who had walked or wanted to train to walk the Camino. I became an active participant, and when they needed extra help with the chapter's social media pages, I volunteered to help manage the event pages and posts. I am still a walk leader for our chapter. Eric and our dog, Sorrento, often meet me for beer and pizza with the other walkers after our treks.

A great benefit of serving in a way that is unique to you is that you will meet others of like mind. They may know someone to introduce you to, or you may even meet a man with similar interests in a very natural and easy way. There are many ways to devote yourself to something greater than yourself.

# Expand Your Comfort Zone to Include Meeting More Men

―❤―

*"You can choose courage, or you can choose comfort.*
*You cannot have both."*
~ Brene Brown

On my journey to love, I needed to reassess my habits and patterns. I realized that I was involved in activities and hobbies that I enjoyed, but that were only sometimes ones that a man might also enjoy. I was an active yoga student, walker, and retreat goer, and I enjoyed dinners out with my girlfriends.

As a solo traveler, I often booked exotic trips related to yoga and wellness. I could travel alone and arrive at a community-centered gathering where meals were shared, and I could do fun activities with other like-minded women. I was very comfortable in that world.

A friend who owned a successful dating service reminded me that I needed to try new things and take on some new hobbies where more men would be participating. She recommended that I spend one month trying four new things a week. When you do the math, that was sixteen new experiences in a month. I tried new things, such as taking a new route to work and stopping for coffee in a different café. I spent a day snorkeling in a cove off the coast and attended local concerts. Thinking up new things to try invigorated my creativity and sense of adventure. My friends coined that time as the *"Summer of Maria."*

I like art museums and music, so I started to attend lectures and concerts on my own. Then, I began to consider what other activities I could engage in where I might meet more men. I joined a singles hiking club and signed up for the occasional day hike and a few overnight events. I lived near a harbor, so I decided to try sailing. I joined a sailing group and had a great summer spending Saturdays on day sails. These experiences pushed me out of my comfort zone and put me on a path of meeting new people with new opportunities.

It is no surprise that synchronicity was at play when I met Eric on a boat after making a conscious decision to try new activities that have a higher percentage of men participating. Eric and I still like to sail together, and we found out we have several other things in common, such as a love of walking, hiking, and traveling.

Dating coach Jacki Sabourin has a robust YouTube channel that teaches and models ways to interact with men. She uses examples of taking the opportunity to talk to men, whether in line at the grocery store, at the gym, or in an elevator. Her advice encourages making eye contact and saying something like, *"So, how is your day going?"* It is a great and simple way to open a dialogue with any stranger. Putting this advice into practice really pushed me out of my comfort zone and lifted my self-confidence. It does take courage, but the results can be astounding.

# Nice Men Know
## Other Nice Men

❤

*"It's not a woman's job to keep a man interested.
It's only her job to know that she is worthy of interest."*
~ Charles J. Orlando

In the years leading up to meeting my husband, I listened to many a love expert. Someone along the way mentioned that nice men know other nice men and that those nice men could be a good resource for meeting other good men. So, I took that advice and asked the married manager at my yoga studio, who I thought was a good man, if he had any single friends. He took my request to heart and fixed me up with a friend of his.

I spoke on the phone with this new prospect and set a date at a nice restaurant overlooking the ocean in Laguna Beach. He brought me flowers and paid for lunch, and then we went on a little walk along the coast. He was a lovely man. Though the gesture of bringing me flowers was very sweet and gentlemanly, I felt awkward receiving them, especially carrying a bouquet around with me on our walk.

Looking back, I see now that it was more about my being unable to receive. Up until that point, my familiar scenario was being involved with men who left me a few crumbs of kindness that I devoured and, like a beggar, waited for any more that may be dropped my way. At that time, I was not ready or feeling worthy of a nice man who would treat me well. I canceled our next date.

Fast forward a few years. Six months into dating Eric, on New Year's morning, we were out of eggs. Eric loves making a hearty breakfast, so he ran to the store after bringing me coffee in bed. He returned with eggs and a bouquet of sunflowers displayed in a vase. I did not see the flowers right away, but when I finally did, my jaw dropped. I was both stunned and delighted. This was the first time he had given me flowers. A shift had occurred within me. I was finally ready to accept flowers from a lovely man who treated me well. Eric continues to bring home flowers as each bouquet needs replacing.

Who are the good men in your life? They might be a family member, colleague, or friend. Have the courage to let them know you want to meet a good quality man. Ask them to please keep you in mind if they have any friends to introduce you to. Have your list of desired characteristics to share with any of your novice matchmakers. A man given a clear mission will usually do whatever it takes to fulfill that mission successfully. As the highest authority of your life, you always reserve the right to say yes or no to the opportunity.

I have also spent time reflecting on the different men who have been in my life. Looking back, I realized that I had many good men who liked me, but I kept them in my friend zone. They did not fit the mold of whom I was generally attracted to. I thought it was my responsibility to keep a man interested and that I had to do all the work. As a result, a good man who showed up for me and had the potential to love me just as I was—without needing to change anything—remained invisible to me. Is there a man you have put in your friend zone who deserves another look as a romantic partner?

# Gratitude Raises Your Vibration and Helps You Meet Your Man

*"Love wholeheartedly, be surprised, give thanks and praise_
then you will discover the fullness of your life."*
~ David Steindl-Rast

I have kept a journal off and on since grade school. The month before I met Eric, my journal turned into a Gratitude Journal. Because I was so focused on gratitude, my vibration was very high when I met him. Since we are a vibrational match to what we attract, I highly recommend keeping your vibration and energy as positive and high as you can—not just for attracting love but for everything else you desire.

Here are some snippets from my journal after meeting Eric:

Wow! 3-Day Ocean Adventure! I am so grateful to have survived, LOL!

Insights:

- I felt utterly vulnerable. Because I was sick, I had to let people take care of me. No masks, removed identity, felt RAW.
- Moving through seasickness to get to the other side. Not sure I would recover but I did!

- I moved through it and came out on the other side, which was more beautiful, enchanting, loving, romantic, and peaceful.
- The child in me remained fascinated and in joy over sunsets, stars, dolphins, and whales.
- I am grateful for Eric G., my partner, my teacher, and my new friend.
- I am grateful for Eric's gentle and Zen-like teaching style.
- I am grateful for Eric's integrity, kindness, patience, and humor.
- I am grateful for Eric's generosity and willingness to hold my hair and sit with me when I was sick.
- I am grateful Eric calls me "La Reina: The Queen!"

Not only was my vibration extremely high, but I found myself completely out of my comfort zone, needing to let go and receive. Nothing felt familiar, so I had to surrender to the process and the experience. My ego lost all control, and I almost passed out; it was terrible, but then my authentic adventurous spirit emerged. At this point, I still did not know what would happen with Eric in the future, if anything, but I remained focused on what I appreciated about him and what I was grateful for in the overall experience.

Studies from major institutions like UCLA and Harvard prove the health benefits of gratitude. Being thankful reduces depression, stress, and anxiety and improves overall health, well-being, and happiness. My husband often tells me how much fun I am to be with because I am generally happy and upbeat. Even in the midst of challenges, I try to see the positive or the lesson in the situation.

With regular practice, focusing on gratitude will become a habit. Eventually, your neuropathways will create a new in-road that becomes familiar and the default in your brain's operating system.

# Prepare for Him
## Through Prayers, Mantras, and Songs

❧

*"Sat patim dehi parameshwara,*
*Om shrim shriyei namaha."*
~ Sanskrit Love Mantra

The above is a Sanskrit mantra from India meant for a woman to attract a love partner.

Prayers, mantras, and songs have a way of cutting through the mind chatter to shift your vibration. If you sing or physically move to it, it has even more potential to create new neuropathways in support of receiving great love.

Sat patim dehi parameshwara translates to, "Please give to me a man who embodies the perfect masculine principles." Om shrim shriyei namaha translates to "Om and Salutations to the creative abundance that is the very form of the Universe." Deva Premal has a beautiful version of this on her album, *Songs for the Inner Lover.*

We have all heard ourselves or someone else express being unlucky in love. When I was single, I decided to take that phrase, turn it around, and make it my own by creating a musical ditty I could dance to: "I am lucky in love, I am lucky in love." It's harder to share the words on paper, but imagine it as a dance cheer.

Below is a prayer I wrote to attract true love:

"Dear God, Goddess, Beloved,

I have a longing deep within the recesses of my soul to be with another in this lifetime. The desire is so great that I am willing to do whatever needs to be done to receive my true love. It would be such an honor to love another in such a deep and holy way. Please help me to heal the parts within that prevent me from being open to and attracting great love. Help me to remove the barriers I keep around me that create obstacles to love. I know I have the potential to be a loving partner to my perfect mate. Please ready my heart for the great love I pray for. Help me to be the woman I need to be to attract true love. So be it, so it is."

Do you have any resistance to utilizing prayer to help manifest your beloved? As Rev. Michael Beckwith of Agape International Spiritual Center teaches, *"Prayer is the foundation of spiritual practice. In its simplest form and expression, prayer awakens your awareness of your Oneness with the Divine. It is the direct channel and line of communication that extends from you to the Heart-Mind of Spirit, of the Presence of the Living God."*

Desiring to be in a loving relationship is a sacred longing worthy of prayer. It is a wonderful thing to bring even more love into the world.

*Love Practices*

# Section Three

## Journal Reflection

What things are you passionate about?

Is there a local non-profit looking for volunteers?

Where might you fill a need that would expose you to new people and experiences and be exciting for you?

How might you show up for others in a way that is unique to you?

Take time to write down things you are grateful for from past relationships, the things you learned, and the positive experiences that you would love more of.

After every date, consider at least one thing you liked about the experience or the person, even if there is no second date.

## Inspired Action

What new hobbies might interest you where men are likely to be?

The following are some examples you could try:

- Go to a new coffee shop, restaurant, or lunch spot.
- Consider taking up golf or a sailing class (they attract men!)

- Dress to the nines, sit at a bar you have never been to, and order a drink and an appetizer. Make eye contact and say, *"Hello, how is your day going so far?"* to those sitting near you.
- Join singles-related events for travel, hiking, or dinners.

If you are feeling low or impatient because your beloved partner seems to be absent, create a song playlist that can positively shift your vibration.

# Mindfulness/Meditation

When you wake in the morning, before opening your eyes, thank God for giving you another day to enjoy your life fully.

Write your own heartfelt prayer for a great love, or borrow mine. Recite it upon waking in the morning and before you fall asleep at night, knowing that your prayer has already been answered and is on its way.

Repeat this affirmation throughout the day:

"I am worthy of interest and love. I am ready to be loved, cherished, and adored."

# Section Four

## CRAFTING YOUR VISION

*"It doesn't interest me what you do for a living.
I want to know what you ache for
and if you dare to dream of meeting your heart's longing."*

Oriah Mountain Dreamer ~ "The Invitation"

# A Season, A Reason...
## Not Necessarily a Lifetime

*"Sometimes you've got to walk away*
*from something to walk into better things."*
~ Temi O'Sola

For quite some time, I lived in what may be called a dry spell when it came to love and romance. Looking back now, I see I shut down that part of me out of self-preservation. Because I could not trust myself to make good decisions about men and dating, I focused instead on my career. I made peace that it was better to be a happy spinster than suffer continuous broken hearts.

Somewhere between my conscious decision to prepare for love and meeting Eric, an exciting and yummy experience found its way to me. Through a series of synchronistic events, I met a man who lived in another state but was visiting his family within walking distance of my apartment. We ended up having a year-long romance as he came to town for different holidays. It was a surprise. It was fun. It was romantic. It was juicy and delicious. It was just what I needed and did not know I wanted.

A part of me knew this relationship was a reason or a season type of connection, but the oxytocin bonding hormone wanted it to be more and produced visions and desires of a future with him.

When I finally accepted that he was not Mr. Lifetime, I ended it. I went through a grieving period that allowed me to engage in some of the practices outlined in "Section Two: Healing Your Love Wounds."

Looking back, I do not regret the choice to have a lover. I had been so disconnected from my sensual and sexual needs and desires that he helped me to reconnect with that part of me. I could also see that while it may have led to another disappointment and heartache, I was in a better place. It was the first relationship where I was not obsessed with the addictive ways I had been in the past. I felt I could be completely myself. He was not my lifetime man, but I was certainly getting closer.

It is possible to attract the gift of a practice run. You may have a few more lessons to learn or things to heal before your forever man can show up. Enjoy what you can, but do not hold on to something for longer than it serves, especially if you know you want your lifetime man. The next chapters will help you get clear on how to manifest your beloved.

# Your Burning Desire...
## For True Love's Kiss

---

*"Be willing to dream, and imagine yourself becoming all
that you wish to be. If you live from those imaginings,
the universe will align with you in bringing all that you wish for—
and even more than you imagined..."*
~ Wayne Dyer

You have admitted to yourself and others that you desire to be with the love of your life. You decided that you are willing to do whatever it takes to bring this desire into reality. Now is the time to dream up a relationship you would absolutely love and put it in writing. Ask yourself, *"What would I love my relationship to be like?"*

Focus on the qualities you desire in a partner. For example, you love how he always treats strangers with kindness even when no one is looking. Instead of being overly focused on physical attributes, be grateful that you are both experiencing vibrant, dynamic health, love walking in nature, and enjoy eating fresh, healthy food. Also, focus on how you want to feel when you are with him. You feel loved, cherished, and adored. You love feeling like you can be 100% yourself when you are with him and how much fun you have together.

Add things that you love doing together with imaginative detail. Describe what a weekend getaway could look like with him. Is it a wine-tasting tour? Is it going to a cabin in the woods for a cozy rustic experience? Or do you like being in big cities and experiencing the restaurant scene and nightlife? Are you someone who likes outdoor summer concerts, sporting events, or cooking new recipes? What does that look like with a romantic partner?

Write out your dream life with your beloved as though it has already happened. It can be as long or as short as you wish. It is also a living vision that can be updated and adjusted at any time. You can envision one year or three years from now as if everything has worked out. Start with, *"I am so happy and grateful now that..."*

Below is an example to get you started:

"I am so happy and grateful now that I am a happily married woman. I am delighted that I am now with my best friend, partner, and lover. We have so much fun together, whether we are doing laundry or traveling through Europe. I love how he makes me laugh. Sunday is my favorite day when we go out to breakfast, sit at a café, and people-watch as we dream up our next travel adventure. Then, we head to the farmers market to pick up local ingredients for our Sunday dinner..."

Create your dream vision and end with *"this or something greater still."* You can start with a paragraph and eventually end up with four pages.

# Live As If...
## It is Even Better Than You Imagined

———❤———

*"Imagine it; live as if it were your reality;*
*allow no detractors; but most important,*
*assume the feeling of it, and you will merge with it and it*
*will merge with you so that it is no longer a duality —*
*it is you becoming one with what you desire."*
~ Wayne Dyer

In the previous chapter, you were asked to create your vision and write it out in exact detail and descriptive language so you could really experience what your life with your beloved would be like.

Now, I want you to take smaller sections of that vision and feel into them—feel them as if they are real and are happening right now. Imagine a vignette you see with your love. I used to lie in bed in the morning before I would open my eyes and imagine that my man was in the kitchen making coffee. I could hear the kettle boiling and the cups clanking, and I smelled freshly ground beans wafting through the house. I felt into this vision as if it were happening in that moment. And guess what? I manifested a man who makes our coffee in the morning and brings me my cup in bed! That is how powerful this practice can be.

I helped my friend Ginnie come up with her vignette. Since she wanted to be in a relationship by the holidays, her vision was of showing up with her new boyfriend at the family party. She felt into how it would feel when she brought her new man to meet her family. She imagined him getting her a glass of wine, then felt him stand next to her with his arm around her waist while they chatted with different family members about how they met. Well, this past holiday season, not only did she bring her man to the family party, but he brought his mom and his daughter to meet Ginnie's side of the family.

Eric and I were in a committed relationship for many years before he asked me to marry him. I wanted to be married but was not sure when it would happen. I had a desire to walk down the aisle to Van Morrison's "*Tupelo Honey*." I would listen to the recording with my eyes closed and see myself in a white dress, holding a beautiful bouquet of white roses, daisies, and baby's breath. I would see my groom ahead, waiting for me, and all my guests standing and beaming at me as I slowly walked down the aisle, taking it all in.

As it turned out, three weeks before my actual wedding, I found a musician who sang "*Tupelo Honey*." There is a video of me hearing the first chords with a huge smile on my face, reacting joyfully to my dream come true. I slowly walked towards my beloved, and our guests stood beaming as I took it all in.

It is essential to be a vibrational match to your dream; living as if and *feeling* as if it is really happening right now is a powerful practice. I had a group of friends who would play a game we called "Feel it Real" with me. For instance, I bought a fake engagement ring that looked real. We would gather for lunch or happy hour, and I would talk about my fiancé as if I really had one. My friends would show up in the vibration of whatever they wanted to manifest at the time as well. Do you have a trusted friend who is willing to play this with you? Call her up and chat with her about your new love as if it is happening right now.

# Must Love Dogs...
## Draw Your Line in the Sand

─━❤━─

*"Intentions compressed into words enfold magical power."*
~ Deepak Chopra

*Must Love Dogs* is a 2005 romantic comedy film based on a novel of the same name. It was produced during the early days of internet dating. Now, it is the cultural norm in the Western world for singles to go online or to an app, create a profile with photos, and write a brief synopsis of who they are and what they are looking for. The things that are important to you must be listed in your profile upfront so that if someone does not align with what is important to you, they can take themselves out of the running and vice versa.

Like many women I hear from who do not like online dating because it feels so unnatural, I, too, had an aversion to it. My philosophy was, and still is, that I wanted to provide the Universe with every avenue for bringing my beloved to me. So, I created an online profile, communicated with men, went on dates, and stayed open to the possibility of meeting my man in this way. I updated my profile from time to time and posted photos that I liked to represent me best. Though I did meet Eric in real life, prior to meeting him, I could never have guessed the synchronistic way he would be brought into my life.

Below is an example of my online profile, which I updated right before meeting Eric.

Here is what I wrote for my dating profile:

"Amazing woman seeking smart, incredible man with a strength of heart and passion for life to match my own. Chicago native born and bred with Midwestern values and pioneer spirit, I came to California two decades ago with two suitcases and $1000 to "seek my fortune." Guess what I discovered? ME!

I love travel, long-distance walking, yoga, British mysteries, and dinner with friends. I just returned from two months in Spain, having walked five hundred miles on the Camino de Santiago. I love summertime in Laguna Beach, enjoying local bands at the Sawdust Festival. I prefer spending my money on experiences, not necessarily things. How about you?

As much as I love to travel, I love the comforts of home, quiet mornings over coffee, and sweet contemplation of the blessings in my life. I am grateful to live within walking distance of the ocean for my evening treks. The Southern California life suits my healthy, active lifestyle, love of beach life, and local organic food. I enjoy cooking for those I love, but if you love to cook, I love to eat!

I am smart, sexy, fun, spiritual, adventurous, positive, and upbeat. I am ready to share my life with an extraordinary man of integrity and humor who loves his life and is healthy, active, and physically fit so we can walk together in the amazing and adventurous life that we co-create.

What inspires you? I can't wait to hear all about it."

When I review this, I see that I was setting an intention and being clear about who I am and what I am looking for. Though Eric never read this, it feels like I sent my order to the Universe, and it was delivered in perfect time.

Eric definitely came with a dog. They did and still do everything together. Although I have never seen an online profile written by Eric, I am sure it would have stated, *"Must love dogs."* If I had not been open to dogs or allergic to them, this would not have been a good fit. Luckily, I love Sorrento, he loves me, and we make a great family of three.

# Keep the Faith...
## Even When He Seems Nowhere in Sight

───────❤───────

*"Hold your vision relentlessly, and more than that—*
*live each day as if that idea you have in your imagination is,*
*in fact, your reality."*
~ Wayne Dyer

I know that the journey to meeting your beloved can seem over-whelming and disheartening at times. I know this road. I was on it too. Now, I am with my beloved husband, Eric. If you feel like this can never happen for you, I am here to tell you with great conviction that it is totally possible because if it can happen for me, it can happen for you. It does take commitment and a personal awareness of where you are in your life, along with clarity about what you desire. I was headed in the entirely opposite direction of a loving relationship and had to shift my focus, or I knew I would never manifest the man I felt I was meant to be with.

If you are reading this book, I know you have sent your rockets of desire and prayers to the Universe: *"Please bring my Love to me!"* Know that your prayer has already been answered. Now, it is your job to remove the barriers, resistance, and beliefs that are keeping you from this desire. You need to be a vibrational match to your dream and know that the Universe is conspiring to deliver it to you.

71

When I moved back to California from the Las Vegas desert, I sent a powerful rocket of desire to the Universe. *"If I am moving back, then I am living by the ocean!"* While searching for an apartment, I struggled to find the perfect place that I loved and could afford. Doubts crept in, and I worried that living by the ocean was not going to work out. One of my spiritual counselors reminded me that it was like ordering a bike and waiting for it to arrive. I had already placed my order and declaration to the Universe; I just needed to let go, focus on my life, and trust that it was on its way. As it turned out, I manifested an amazing one-bedroom apartment with a 180-degree view of the ocean for an incredibly fixed rent, where I lived for many years.

Manifesting uses the same universal laws, whether it is for an apartment or your true love. However, there may be more resistance to love based on past experiences than manifesting an apartment. So, keep the faith. I know this is possible for you, and I will hold that vision for you.

# Love Practices

## Section Four

# Journal Reflection

Light a candle to set the stage for this beautiful unfolding.

Set aside at least an hour of time and space to craft your vision.

Focusing on things you are grateful for or listening to upbeat music can help you reach a higher vibrational state.

Start to write out what you would love in your dream relationship. What do you want to experience? How do you want to feel when you are with your man?

# Inspired Action

What would you love to manifest with your man? Is it your wedding day? Is it having a date for the next wedding you are invited to? Is it going away on a romantic weekend getaway?

If you are not online, try at least a 3-month subscription to an online dating app or website.

Write a creative online profile or update your current profile. If you have resistance, enlist the support of a good friend who can help you get in touch with your greatest attributes and what you are looking for in a man.

If you have had a profile up for a time, switch out the photos or consider a professional photo shoot.

## *Mindfulness/Meditation*

After designing a scenario you would love to manifest, take some time each day to sit quietly for about five minutes or play music to enhance the experience. Then, using your imagination and all your positive feelings and emotions, feel into it as if it is happening right now. Read your vision daily. If you have crafted a four-page vision, read that once a week. Then, glean a smaller size version, about a paragraph, that you can keep in your wallet to read daily.

Have a trusted friend who will remind you that your dream is important. That you have sent your order to the Universe, and you are simply waiting for it to be delivered.

# Section Five

## PILGRIMAGE, PRAYER, AND SPANISH RICE

*"A pilgrimage is a journey, often into an unknown or foreign place, where a person goes in search of new or expanded meaning about themselves, others, nature, or higher good through the experience. It can lead to a personal transformation, after which the pilgrim returns to their daily life."*

~Maria Mugica

# Buen Camino!
## Good Journey to You!

———◆———

*"Desire is not what causes suffering.*
*It is the attachment to desire that steals our joy.*
*Desire what your heart desires, and then get out of your own way.*
*Detach from your desire and continue to do what makes you happy.*
*When it resurfaces in your thoughts, feel the joy of already having it,*
*and also the peace of knowing that what is meant for you*
*will never pass you by."*
~ Sama Akbar

A few years back, I turned a layoff from work into a sabbatical and fulfilled some key items on my bucket list. I finally had time for yoga teacher certification training, went on a 500-mile walking pilgrimage across Spain on the Camino de Santiago, and, upon my return, met my man. There is something to be said for the commitments you make to yourself and your journey. We do it because we must fulfill the longing of our Souls without knowing the outcome.

The Camino de Santiago, also known as the Way of St. James, is a network of pilgrimage routes that lead to the tomb of Saint James the Greater in the Cathedral of Santiago de Compostela in Spain. The Camino is a UNESCO World Heritage Site. Many writers and celebrities have documented their experiences on the Camino in books and films, including Paulo Coelho, Shirley MacLaine, Martin Sheen, and Emilio Estevez. It continues to grow in popularity. While many go for religious or spiritual reasons, many also go for the cultural and physical aspects of the journey. I had felt called to go for about thirteen years prior to finally having the time and will to commit to a journey of this magnitude.

Reflecting on my journey, I now believe that my pilgrimage across Spain was the final step in my preparation for meeting my husband Eric. Although my pilgrimage taught me many lessons, one of the most significant takeaways was learning to love without attachment. Each person has a distinct experience of what is often referred to as the Camino, and if you decide to walk it, you will meet many other pilgrims along the Way. Deep and meaningful conversations and connections with others are common, as the most frequently asked question on the Camino is, *"Why are you here?"* This existential question deserves the time needed to hear each pilgrim's response. When you are walking twelve to fifteen miles a day for over forty days, there is plenty of time.

I met pilgrims who were there for the adventure and others who had felt called for many years. A mom empty-nester was trying to remember who she was without her kids. One man was carrying his brother's ashes to scatter across the ocean at Finisterre. Another mother was walking in memory of her son, who had walked the Camino before his sudden death shortly after returning home. Many were in transition after a job loss, like me, and some because of the ending of a relationship. Even those who came for no spiritual or existential reasons still felt it to be a profound and transformational experience.

In this unique and special journey, I found myself falling into loving with so many of my fellow pilgrims. There were times when I would walk side by side with someone for an hour, a day, a few days, or even a month. At some point, they may have had to go ahead or stay behind because their time was limited, or they had to return home. I had such deep and meaningful conversations with some of the fellow pilgrims that I desired to spend the entire forty-plus days with them, yet I knew they had their timelines and journeys to complete. I had to let them go while remaining appreciative of the time we had.

In the past, when a relationship ended, I was in great suffering and despair. It felt so painful that I would find myself shutting down and wanting to give up on love. Upon reflection, I wonder, what if I had loved that former lover without attachment or a belief that this needed to last forever or fulfill all my needs? Then, I might have been able to part ways lovingly focused on the gratitude that I was able to spend the time along the way with them. What if we could say, *"Buen Camino—good journey to you,"* in all ways that things, people, and situations come to an end?

# The Power of Prayer:
## Life is Better Shared

———❤———

Oh Great Father/Mother God,
Please send my love to me.
From across the sea
And over the mountain,
May he travel to my side.
And then, dear Lord,
When he arrives at my house,
May the food he finds here make him strong
I await his coming.
I prepare my things.
Please ready my heart.
Amen.
Marianne Williamson ~ "Enchanted Love"

I carried the prayer above in my backpack on my pilgrimage across Spain on the Camino de Santiago. While I cannot say that this was "the" thing that brought me to Eric, I do believe it was part of my process and part of the collective work I did to prepare for his arrival. However, the unique events that brought us together have made me wonder about its synchronicity.

In the previous chapter, I mentioned one of my biggest takeaways from walking the Camino was loving without attachment. Another significant realization was that life, the journey, is better shared. I left for the Camino alone and had no expectations of walking with others. However, the Way had other plans for me. Around day four, I met up with my rag-tag team of pilgrims, who became my companions for the rest of my walk. We experienced the highs and lows together. When, at times, I was not sure if I could physically continue, they supported me and cheered me on. I did the same for them. Being witnessed or witnessing others is an enriching part of the human journey.

One month after returning from Spain, Eric and I met on a boat in San Francisco Bay. Eric lived in the mountains of Southern California, and I lived by the ocean. We traveled separately to San Francisco Bay, and our journey brought us down along the coast of California to Long Beach. While the metaphor for food in the prayer above may be more about being nourished by a loving relationship, food is an essential component of our lives. Eric loves to cook and try new recipes, yet feels very nourished when I prepare a simple meal for us. For me, *"Please ready my heart."* was the most essential part of the prayer. I needed to be ready to receive the gift of my prayer.

Prayer helps you set your intention. Then, let go and turn it over to God. Holding the vision, know that it is already done. Your prayer is answered even though you cannot see it in physical reality just yet. My prayer was amplified by being on a pilgrimage, a sacred journey. Say your prayers in the morning and the evening, then go about your business.

# Granny's Spanish Rice
## Seals the Deal for Love

———❤———

"In two tablespoons of oil, brown one cup of rice. Skim
oil. Add ½ a can of tomato sauce, approximately four
ounces. Add 2.5 cups of boiling water with bouillon.
Add a large slice of onion and garlic to taste.
Cover and simmer for approximately a half hour."
~ Maria Victoria Mugica, aka Granny

Shortly after returning from Spain, I was longing for another
adventure. A captain friend had put out a request to assist him
in bringing a boat from San Francisco to San Pedro near Long
Beach. I felt called to join this next journey. Though I was not an
avid sailor, I called him and told him I was game and to tell me
what to do. He agreed, and two weeks later, I was flying up to San
Francisco Bay, where I joined a small crew that consisted of my
captain friend, his girlfriend, and this man named Eric. Eric and I
were partnered up and shared the V-birth, as well as the 11:00 pm-
2:00 am shift and 5:00 am- 8:00 am shift, as we needed to drive
the boat through the night.

We set sail at about 4:00 a.m., and it was so cold. My longjohns, hat,
and heavy windbreaker were not enough to keep out the chill of this
July San Francisco Bay morning. At that time of day, all I was eating
were cookies and instant coffee.

When we left the bay and encountered the ocean waves, the boat was tossed around, and everything began to spill out of cabinets and off shelves. The mini fridge emptied its contents onto the floor. The captain was trying to steady the boat while Eric was sent above to secure the propane tanks that were rolling about. The other crew member was on the floor collecting all the items that were being thrown around. I was hanging on for dear life, trying not to faint as everything crashed down around me. I remember feeling faint, but I stopped myself because I knew there was no one there to take care of me afterward.

At some point, I was about to lose my cookies, so I went out to the back of the boat and puked into the wind. I was not anticipating that it would blow back in my face, hair, and clothes. This happened a couple of times when Eric came out to check on me and offered to hold my hair. Needless to say, I was a mess. I was seasick the whole day and not much help. However, Eric continued to keep an eye on me and take care of me.

That evening marked our first shift from 11:00 pm to 2:00 am. My legs felt weak, and I could only keep down pretzels and sparkling water. Fortunately, Eric was an avid sailor and was okay with being paired with a seasick, unskilled, land-loving woman. It was pitch dark, and the electronics, along with the wheel and rudder, were temperamental at best. We had quite a ride that night. Along the way, he asked, *"Do you, by any chance, have a good Spanish rice recipe?"* The funny thing is, I did have a great Spanish rice recipe. My Granny, who came from Mexico to the US during the Mexican Revolution, had a recipe that everyone in our family keeps in their collection.

I tried to recall the recipe and verbally share it with Eric but could not remember it exactly. Finally, I told him that I would ask my mom to send it when we were back on land. We carried on with the rest of the journey, occasionally referencing the recipe. After the boat docked in San Pedro and we started to collect our things to return to our regularly scheduled lives, Eric had made no indications of getting together except to get my Granny's recipe. As we departed, I went in for a hug, which he reciprocated.

Our captain had us all on an email chain, so when I got home, knowing Eric was getting home much later, I sent him an email that read, *"Howdy Partner, hoping you made it home safely. Recipe coming soon!"* and my phone number. The next day, he texted me hello and requested the recipe again. I had my mom send it to me, and I forwarded it to him.

We texted over a couple of days, and he shared his progress on making Spanish Rice. A day or so after that, he called and asked me out on a date. Granny's recipe became the focal point for connection after the adventure, and we still enjoy eating it to this day.

To celebrate and embody this chapter, try Granny's Spanish Rice Recipe above. Serve with black beans, grilled vegetables, shredded cheese, and salsa in your favorite tortilla. As you sit down to eat, give a toast to all those who have found love. Then declare, *"I'm next!"*

# Can't I Love Just a Little Bit?

*"Embracing vulnerability involves acknowledging
and accepting our own limitations and imperfections.
It requires us to confront our fears, insecurities, and mistakes.
By doing so, we cultivate self-awareness
and learn to embrace our "true self."
This acceptance frees us from the burden of pretending to be perfect
and allows us to focus on personal growth and self-improvement."*
~ Jeremy Grandstaff

When I met Eric at sea, I was so out of my element. Not only was I not an avid sailor, but I was also overcome with seasickness. The strong, confident woman who had just walked 500 miles across Spain was a pathetic mess. I had to rely on the help and support of my sailing partner. All my masks and walls were down. I could no longer pretend to have it all together.

I had been disappointed by love so many times that I had built up some thick walls. I wanted to fall in love but was so afraid of getting hurt. I remember asking a spiritual teacher if it was possible to love just a little bit. In essence, I asked, *"Can I open my heart a little, see if the coast is clear and safe, and then love fully?"* She laughed gently, knowing that is just not how it works.

If we truly respect ourselves, others around us cannot help but show respect. With awareness, we can create healthy boundaries in relationships. Yet, the heart wants what the heart wants. Sometimes, it just explodes with love for another. This is what we cannot help or control.

Years prior to meeting Eric, my armored heart and I would sometimes get asked out on dates. On one date, I happened to mention, with some attitude, that I did not need a man. Looking back now, I see that I took the offensive protective posture. My inner protector was trying to save me because deep down, I believed that he could ultimately disappoint and break my heart. I am sure it is no surprise there was not a second date.

Eric is such a helpful person. Like many men, he is wired to come to the rescue when needed. Every day of our three-day adventure at sea, I needed help. I found the boat hard to steer, and I would get nervous. Then, I would shout, *"Eric, help!"* And he would come to help me. Even in my pathetic messiness, he still somehow saw me as a strong, confident woman and continues to believe that to this day.

Did the Universe conspire to set us up? I think, yes. In the past, I was so afraid of being vulnerable and depending on others that I pushed many friends, family, lovers, and nice men away. One of the final steps to attracting a loving partnership for me was being vulnerable. To have someone come to look for me because I was puking off the back of a boat is a very vulnerable position to be in. I was too much in need to keep up the walls of protection.

Now, I do not expect anyone reading my story to set themselves up by throwing themselves out to sea to create a vulnerable or dangerous moment, hoping someone would come to the rescue. However, you can consider how you can be open and authentic on dates by honestly sharing your heart's desire. Suppose you are in the beginning stages of dating someone, and you know that you want to be married one day or have children. In that case, it is important to share that sooner rather than later so you do not waste precious time, especially if your date has no interest in either.

My practice of vulnerability continues through the writing of this book. I have been sharing my triumphs, failures, and lived experiences. I am sharing things that may surprise some of the people who have known me all my life.

# A Courting We Will Go

*"Wait for someone who kisses your forehead, who wants to show you off to the world when you are in track pants, who will hold your hand in front of his friends, who thinks you are just as pretty without makeup. One who is constantly reminding you of how much he cares."*
~ Unknown Author

My wish for you is that you may experience a sweet courtship if you so desire. I chose to add a section on courtship because before meeting Eric, I did not know what courtship could look like. I knew what I had seen in the movies or read in Jane Austen novels, but what could it look like in the life of a modern independent woman? As a recovering "fiercely" independent woman, being courted by Eric was a joy and delight. I did not realize how much I craved sweetness.

Each courtship will look different as each couple is unique. However, there are common gestures and characteristics of courting. From the beginning, Eric made coming to see me a priority. He lived ninety minutes away in the mountains, and I lived by the ocean. He was willing to drive to me on the weekend and plan things that he knew would make me happy. He was committed to me very early on and was the one to start calling me his girlfriend within the first couple of months. I never had to wonder or ask, *"Where is this going?"* Introductions to his family came within the first few months.

Being courted was a new experience for me. I was not used to receiving flowers, hand-painted postcards, being escorted across the street, or having doors held open for me. I received auto repair support and much loving care. It felt as though he thought of everything—which he did!

My friend Ginnie started dating a divorced man with a teenage daughter. The man consistently showed up for Ginnie, followed through with plans, and called when he said he would. However, he said he wanted time before he had Ginnie meet his daughter. This was challenging at times for Ginnie, as she wanted more reassurance in the early stages and felt that not meeting his family meant she was not important enough.

When Ginnie would get nervous that things were not progressing as she was hoping they would, she had me and other trusted friends remind her of the progress that was happening and to be patient and trust the right timing. Eventually, she met his side of the family. Open dialogue and trusting the process will help you in all stages of courtship and dating.

When you are with the right person, courtship can be effortless and delightful. While there was a newness in the early stages of our relationship, Eric continues to court me in our marriage as well. I feel so beloved when he kisses me on the forehead. That gesture is incredibly intimate and makes me feel cherished beyond measure.

# Love Practices

## Section Five

## Journal Reflection

———❤———

In your journal, write out your heart's desires and non-negotiables when dating that are best shared sooner rather than later.

Reflect in your journal if there is something in your desire for love that feels entirely out of reach.

Are there parts inside of you that feel you may not be worthy of interest or pursuit?

You can create an affirmation to replace fear and self-doubt, such as, *"I am worthy of great love because I am a child of God, and I am great at loving myself and others."* To help integrate the affirmation more deeply, you can add the breathing practice from the section "Installing New Thoughts."

## Inspired Action

———❤———

You can look for a prayer or create your own. I discuss this and provide examples in "Section Two: Preparing for Him."

How can you cultivate a sense of pilgrimage in your daily life without flying across the world? Is there a peaceful walk near your home, by the ocean, or through a forest that could become your sacred time and walking prayer?

Commit to walking your sacred path consistently, carrying a prayer or affirmation in your pocket, and reciting it as you walk.

# Mindfulness/Meditation

If you have people in your past, whether romantic or not, to whom you still feel attached or have unresolved feelings for, it is not too late to wish them a *"Buen Camino."* If someone comes to mind, take a moment in a quiet space where you will not be interrupted. Visualize them in your mind's eye.

Reflect on the moments you cherished during your time together and the insights you gained about yourself from the relationship. Imagine yourself walking down a beautiful natural path with them. You are talking, laughing, or simply enjoying the tranquility of your surroundings together when you reach a fork in the road. You know which path you will choose, while this person will take the other. At a soul level, you both understand that these are the journeys each of you must pursue for your growth. Face each other and fill your heart with love. Acknowledge that they have their own path to follow. Feel gratitude for the time you shared, hug if appropriate, and wish them well. Allow yourself to experience whatever emotions arise. You might choose to journal about this experience.

# Section Six

## GETTING TO THE CHURCH ON TIME

*"All my life, I thought that the story was over when the hero and heroine were safely engaged—after all, what's good enough for Jane Austen ought to be good enough for anyone. But it's a lie. The story is about to begin, and every day will be a new piece of the plot."*

Mary Ann Shaffer & Annie Barrows
~The Guernsey Literary and Potato Peel Pie Society

# Adaptability is Key
## to a Successful Love Life

———◆———

*"We cannot direct the wind, but we can adjust the sails."*
~ Dolly Parton

Adaptable means to adjust to new conditions. So, for those of you smart, successful, independent women who have been single awhile, a new man in your life has the potential to change everything.

While the first year of courtship with Eric was fun, adventurous, and romantic, it was also a time of adjustment. Before I met my sweetheart, I had been single most of my life. I enjoyed living alone, was described by my friends as fiercely independent, and really liked my bed to myself. It took time to adjust to having a man physically and energetically in my life, not to mention a dog.

Even before meeting my soulmate, I knew that my biggest challenge would be sharing my bed. I was a sensitive sleeper and had suffered bouts of insomnia over the years. I often booked a private room when I traveled with friends or family. So, of course, life's sense of humor helped me manifest a snuggler who loves to roll over, grab me in a full-body bear hug, and take over my entire side of the bed. In the first few months, I definitely had trouble getting a good night's sleep, but the early months were so delicious that sleeplessness was part of the package.

Over time, I realized that I loved him and his sweet embrace more than I loved a bed to myself.

Now, he is part of my sleep routine. I have adapted to sharing a bed, and I use earplugs, an eye mask, and white noise in the background.

When my friend Ginnie was moving in with her new man, she knew that she was much more organized and tidier than him. She considered ahead of time how she might navigate this without being stressed or causing any tension or fights around the subject. She made sure that he had lots of areas to keep his things easily accessible in drawers and closets. Then, monthly, they agreed to spend one to two hours going through any piles that start to accumulate to toss or file. So far, cohabitating is going well for them, and they are now talking about marriage.

This is not about asking you to compromise your integrity or non-negotiables; it is about negotiating some comfort zones and routines to make room for your new love.

# Add More Yin to Your Yang:
## Be the Feminine Energy in His Life

*"A woman in harmony with her spirit is like a river flowing.*
*She goes where she will without pretense*
*and arrives at her destination prepared to be herself."*
~ Maya Angelou

I have beautiful, stylish, intelligent, and sophisticated female friends who are single. What I notice is that as beautiful and feminine as they may dress, something in their energy and the way they carry themselves projects a masculine strength. We all have feminine and masculine energy and attributes. We can be in balance with both or embody one more than the other regardless of our gender.

For many years, I embodied more of my masculine energy. It was, in part, a wall of protection after repeated heartbreak and disappointment. It was also how I was trained to be in the world in my male-dominated careers. Masculine energy is how I got s**t done in my life, and I still use it when I need to.

Alison Armstrong, the creator of *Understanding Men and Satisfying Women*, taught me that women are the color in a man's black-and-white world: Our skin is soft, our bodies have curves, and our emotions are wild.

How do we let down our armor, soften into our feminine/yin energy, and shift from push energy to receiving energy? I have friends who have explored pole dancing, boudoir photos, feminine pleasure coaches, and clothing stylists to help connect to their femininity. Have you explored some of these for yourself? This may feel like more of a surface transformation, but it is a great place to start.

My experience with embodying more feminine energy comes from being in tune with my physical body through dance, being in nature, and a gentle yoga practice. Breath work and awareness of my emotions also fall into the realm of a feminine, receptive practice as opposed to a masculine vibration of taking action and doing.

There is a growing awareness among many spiritual female entrepreneurs who are altering the paradigm for themselves and other women regarding how they operate their lives and businesses. They aim to align more closely with the rhythms of nature and their own bodies, rather than succumbing to a hustle mentality. Some of the women I follow in this space include Mama Gena, Jessica Zweig, and Danielle LaPorte. I will share their information in the resource section if you would like to explore them further on your own.

Throughout the journey, take time to uncover the mystery that is you and uncover the blocks you may have put up to stop yourself from being more in your feminine. Some of these blocks may dissolve upon reflection, while others may need more time to be released. As I started to have more positive experiences with men, I began to trust myself in relation to them, and the more comfortable I could be in my feminine energy.

With my husband, it feels like a dance. Sometimes, I take the lead and get a lot done. Then, when I realize I might be coming on too strong, I step back and let him take charge. When I'm in what I call Project Manager Maria mode, I notice my husband pulls back and becomes more resistant. He doesn't need another man in his life; he prefers his colorful goddess.

# The Spell is Broken

*"Once in a while, right in the middle of an ordinary life...*
*Love comes along and brings you a Fairy Tale!"*
~ Mallika Nawal

In many fairy tales, the main characters are often placed under a spell. This may be a sleeping spell that requires true love's kiss to awaken, or it could involve being transformed into a beast until one learns to love and be loved. I was under a spell of my own unconscious creation. A combination of the wiring of my brain, societal conditioning, and my first male interactions with father figures set me up for a pattern that I repeated for decades. As mentioned in a previous chapter, I attracted romantic partners who vanished shortly after they arrived. I did not realize I created this pattern for my safety. I was protecting my heart from heartache; however, it backfired repeatedly.

When I met Eric and we started dating, something felt different. He showed up in ways like no man I had dated before. He was solid, authentic, and reliable. He meant what he said and followed through on his plans and promises.

Somewhere in the first year of dating, Eric was helping me look something up online. We were in the kitchen, and I was on one side of the counter washing dishes. He was on the other side with his laptop, looking at the screen through his reading glasses. I remember gazing at him in wonder and thinking to myself, *"Wow, he is not going anywhere.*" It was a statement, a realization, a deep knowing, and a new experience.

Eric does not sprint from relationship to relationship; he stays the course. My chaotic relationship pattern seemed to be at an end. My running days were over. This was a relationship that could be built on a solid foundation with two people willing to stay the course. However, along the way, life had a test for me. A couple of years into the relationship, things were progressing nicely, and routines were settling in. That was when sneaky thoughts started to infiltrate my mind.

I had thoughts like, *"I manifested this guy; maybe I can manifest someone even* ***more...***"—fill in the blank! After the initial courtship and early romance had passed, I was starting to lose that electric charge of newness. The excitement of new love and the honeymoon phase was fading. My ego-mind was trying to sabotage my happiness. This was not my typical chaotic pattern, so my ego-mind wanted to create some drama. It was seducing me to break up with the best guy I had ever dated.

I was getting close to pulling the trigger for no obvious reason. Fortunately, I confided in a very good friend who had supported me since I consciously started preparing for love. She stopped me in my tracks and reminded me of the road it took to get here and all the work I did to finally meet my man. *And* what a great man I had manifested.

I was beginning to understand what I was doing, yet I hadn't fully changed my direction. Then, perfectly timed, I listened to a podcast about relationships, and I was gobsmacked. A woman was speaking about exactly what I was thinking and how she woke up to her patterns! She recognized what she was doing and shifted her thoughts. She explained how tricky the ego can be. She was accustomed to an old, chaotic pattern rather than a healthy, loving one.

The first step was to become aware of what was happening. Then, she expressed gratitude and focused on what was working in the relationship to move herself in the best direction. With the truth-telling from my good friend and the message in the podcast, I woke up, too. From that day forward, I stayed the course.

When we have turned a corner and finally manifest a long-held dream, we need to be an energetic match to bring it into existence and embody it long enough for it to become a new habit and way of being. The neural pathways are still making new inroads.

According to Gay Hendricks' work, I see now that I was experiencing an upper-limit problem. He describes it as, "Each of us has an inner thermostat setting that determines how much love, success, and creativity we allow ourselves to enjoy. When you exceed your inner thermostat setting, you will often do something to sabotage yourself, causing you to drop back into the old, familiar zone where you feel secure."

With my new awareness, I could see that my ego-mind was trying to sabotage my good to keep me safe. All my old unhealthy patterns were shifting. I was the sleeping princess awaiting true love's kiss. I was the beast learning to love and be loved. With this awakening, the spell was broken. I attracted, chose, and embodied a healthy, loving relationship for the first time in my life. I am the director of my thoughts, the creator of my life, and you are of yours!

# Marriage Is Perfectly Imperfect

*"Love is our true destiny.*
*We do not find the meaning of life by ourselves alone –*
*we find it with another."*
~ Thomas Merton

When fairy tales end with, *"And they lived happily ever after,"* it makes it sound like they do just that. However, I have a hunch that if we really dug into it, couples in fairy tales have communication breakdowns, childhood triggers surface, and some storms to weather.

Happily Ever After *is* a choice that individuals and couples must make every day. It means setting the intention that, no matter what, I want to have the best possible life with you, even when the going gets tough.

As our years together progress, I feel more grounded within the relationship and myself. My friends have reflected that I seem softer, more receptive, and more balanced since meeting Eric. The wedding ceremonies, witnesses, and commitment have created a structure or container for the two of us to reside in.

I am also noticing that some situations between us trigger some of my unhealed wounds from childhood. Sometimes, I play out my old ways of coping, which include wanting to run from the experience, physically and emotionally. Yet even as I go through my reactions, I am with a partner who observes these parts of me, holds space while I unravel, and does not appear to take it personally. He still loves, adores, and accepts me even when I am not being the best version of myself.

Being in a close, intimate partnership has shown me what it is like to be with someone who has my back and is extremely supportive. The relationship also offers a mirror-like reflection of the good, bad, and ugly within me. It shows me the parts of myself that need love, support, and healing. Healing those parts can only come from me.

It starts with awareness—with noticing what is coming up for me. Sometimes, I must forgive myself for the shame and guilt I may feel for not being perfect or for feeling exposed because another person has witnessed some really immature part of me acting out. Learning how to feel my feelings without creating a story around them helps me see that I am not my feelings, but it also does not allow me to bypass the uncomfortableness that the feeling may be producing.

I am a work in progress. This is a work in progress. Our relationship is growing, changing, and evolving. I know that we are both committed to being the best versions of ourselves with each other.

# Love Can Be Inspiring

---♥---

*"The beginning of love is to let those we love be perfectly themselves and not to twist them to fit our own image."*
~ Thomas Merton

I love being married! I love having someone to call my husband. I love having someone I can count on to be by my side in good times and challenging times. And I love living with my plus one for weddings, funerals, work parties, and more. I love having a partner to bounce ideas off of. I love being half of a couple. I love that I have a witness to my life, and I get to witness another.

I am so grateful for the work I did to prepare for Eric and our relationship. There is something to be said for a woman who waits until her fifties to marry. I know myself so much better now than when I was younger. I studied with so many relationship experts, and that changed the way I thought about men and myself in relation to them. For all my longing and discontent when I was single, I am so grateful that the wait finally manifested the perfect person for me.

There are healthy differences between Eric and me, as well as things that dovetail beautifully. An area where I focus more is the spiritual side of life. My spiritual evolution is a very conscious choice and essential to me. I invest regularly in coaches, trainings, workshops, and retreats that support my personal growth. I also invest in alternative health care like acupuncture and chiropractic and take an array of supplements to keep me healthy and in balance.

Eric does not invest in such things and only sometimes agrees with my choices. But he supports me, and we have open and honest conversations about what we each pursue. Eric also invests in his own interests and hobbies. We are fortunate to be a two-income household, so we can make decisions together and separately about how we spend our finances.

While Eric may not identify as a spiritual person, I see him as a very kind and compassionate human who loves being in nature and with the creatures in it. I would describe him as a salt-of-the-earth kind of man who lives a spiritual life by just being.

My husband is the best person to have in your corner when you really need solid support. When my dad was on his deathbed, Eric flew back to Chicago with me. We stayed the night, sharing a hospital bed next to my dad. It was not comfortable, but there was no other option in Eric's mind except to be there by my side.

We both prefer experiences to things. We do not buy each other gifts for holidays and birthdays. We spend our money on travel and culinary delights, among other things. I discovered that my husband was a fantastic travel companion on our honeymoon through Portugal and Spain. He was a great researcher and planner, and he kept us moving even when jet lag was a factor. We both stayed in joyful anticipation of what each leg of the journey would manifest. Being on our honeymoon, strangers, hotel, and restaurant staff had no shortage of generous surprises to celebrate our union.

In the Osho Tarot, there is a card featuring two trees that are separate yet connected by their roots. Their branches extend towards the sky. I love how each tree stands majestically on its own while remaining connected at its roots. It serves as a beautiful metaphor for a healthy relationship in which two people can come together while maintaining their individuality.

My husband loves Formula 1 car racing. On Sunday mornings, we love to lounge in bed, drinking coffee while he watches racing and I read some sacred spiritual text. This is life. This is partnership. Stay open to the possibilities.

If you are reading my book, you may be a woman who describes herself as spiritual and hopes to meet a man who is as well. You may not get the man you expect. He may not be spiritual in the ways you are, but do not judge or rule him out. Look deeper and remember that we are all spiritual beings having a human experience. You want to be aware of how he treats others, whether or not anyone is watching. How is he with his family, children, and strangers? Does he live a life of integrity? Does he treat you with great care and respect?

# Love Practices

## Section Six

## Journal Reflection

———❤———

Write down anything that you envision could be difficult for you to change or adapt in your routines. Can you problem-solve solutions like Ginnie?

What do you believe are the non-negotiables as opposed to what you would be willing to change (adapt) to be embraced by a beautiful relationship?

## Inspired Action

———❤———

Try yoga, especially a gentle practice like Yin Yoga.

Create a music list to dance to or take up belly dancing.

Take time to review your closet and assemble outfits that make you feel more feminine. Alternatively, consider collaborating with a stylist to develop a look that expresses your femininity in ways you love.

Take time for breathwork and meditation.

# Mindfulness/Meditation

Find a quiet space, sit in a relaxed pose, and feel into your physical body. Notice how your feet feel on the floor or in your shoes. Wiggle your toes. Work your way up your legs to your hips, noticing how your clothing feels against your skin or if there is a breeze. Focus on how it feels to be sitting in the chair. Continue to raise your awareness up your body to the top of your head, noticing all the physical sensations along the way.

Now, go back and notice any feelings you may be experiencing in your emotional body without defining or having a story around it. I notice most of my feelings in my solar plexus located above my belly button, as well as around my heart and throat. Observe what you feel or sense without judgment. Sit with it until you feel a shift. The shift can be as subtle as a yawn or a spontaneous deeper breath and a feeling of letting go. I invite you to write down any observations in your journal.

# Section Seven

## WRITE *YOUR* NEW STORY

*"In the land of all possibilities,*
*there must be a possibility where it all works out."*

Mary Morrissey

# Write Your Own Story
## And Write It With Passion!

———❤———

*"Words create worlds."*
~ Abraham Joshua Heschel,
Moral Grandeur and Spiritual Audacity: Essays

Inspirational messages can be found everywhere if you stay open to them. They can even appear on an ordinary roll of paper towels. I was on a writing retreat in Mexico when our facilitator discovered an amazing quote on the roll of paper towels in her casita that declared, *"Escribe tu propia historia y escríbela con pasión!"* ~ *"Write your own story and write it with passion!"*

She searched through the roll for more copies since it contained a variety of quotes; however, it turned out to be the only one with that particular message. Not only did it joyfully meet a synchronicity quota for all of us participants who reveled in this little miracle when the towel was displayed, but it also struck me as an important message to share with you, my readers.

Words are powerful. You have the power to shift your perspective and your future by reframing your narrative. If you have been telling a story of woe regarding love and romance, you can change it right now. The exercises I shared in "Section Four: Crafting Your Vision," got you started, but you can go further by rewriting your life.

Rewriting your life is a process of shifting your perspective and taking action to create a better future. It involves acknowledging your past, learning from it, and moving forward. There are steps you can take to achieve this.

As I mention throughout the book, reflect on your past and your life story. Include the most meaningful moments and events. Include the difficult ones and the joyful ones. After you have identified the most meaningful events, consider what empowering lessons you learned. Can you find gratitude for the difficulties you have overcome? If not, retell your story from a perspective that empowers you.

This may be an important time to practice the forgiveness technique I described in "Section Two: Healing Your Love Wounds." Forgiveness can help you release the past, make peace with what occurred, and allow you to move forward. Once you find yourself in a positive mental, spiritual, and physical space, envision the life you truly desire.

Now it is time to write your new story, "con pasión!" Junie Swadron, author of the book *Re-Write Your Life*, states, "The sweet whisperings of your soul meets you on the page, and something shifts. You strengthen, you begin to stand taller. Then, one day, you begin to notice that your voice on the page has become your voice in the world." That voice is your power to manifest the life of your dreams.

Junie was my coach throughout the process of writing this book, which is part memoir and part guide. I chose to reframe and learn from my past unsuccessful relationships as valuable lessons that reflected how I felt about myself at the time. I also decided to believe that I could change the course of my love life to one that works out. Through commitment, dedication, and a strong desire, I was able to manifest the love of my life. I spoke it, wrote it, and dreamed it into existence.

The following story poured out of me as I transcribed it to the page. Enjoy!

# A Fairy Tale

*Once Upon a Time,* there was a princess who desired to meet the love of her life. But as she grew, she built a wall to guard against what she longed for the most. She had learned that people can hurt and disappoint, so it felt safer to have a wall around herself. That at least ensured protection from pain and heartache but mostly disappointment. Life had taught her enough that this was the truth, and it became her truth. Yet, she was a hopeless romantic. She had been taught, like most young princesses, that the handsome prince would show up and take her away to his kingdom, and they would live happily ever after. All the books she read had similar themes.

When she came of age, she was introduced to many princes. Yet, they all seemed to have tiny kingdoms. She met the Prince of Small-Mindedness, the Prince of Aloofness, and a wounded prince who did not love himself, so he could not love another, especially her, in the ways she required.

After a time, she thought it best to reside in a cottage in the forest where nothing could harm her. She became very good at tending to her own needs so she would not need to rely on others. She spent many years in the comfort and safety of her cottage. She made sure the wall around her garden was high to keep harmful critters out. This worked for her, and she resolved that it was better to be an eccentric spinster princess than an unhappy, compromised queen.

However, there was a voice that she would occasionally hear that told her to lower her garden wall and to stay open to the possibility of meeting the prince she most longed for. Time after time, she ignored the voice until it got so loud that she could no longer ignore it. This voice instructed her to take a journey to a distant land where she would discover the secrets to love.

She prepared for the journey that would require her to walk hundreds of miles to the Land of Dreams Fulfilled. Along "The Way," she met a ragtag team of travelers also seeking the Land of Dreams Fulfilled. With this tribe, she enjoyed much laughter, adventure, and shared meals, along with both physical and mental exhaustion.

Often, she wasn't sure if she would finish the journey. However, it was her tribe that kept her going, as she, too, was, at times, the source of their strength and support. After many days and countless miles, they reached their destination. There, they discovered that the end was truly the beginning. Yet, the greatest truth she found was that a journey of this magnitude was infinitely more meaningful when shared.

She bid farewell to her fellow travelers and returned to her cottage. When she arrived, she noticed how tall the garden wall actually was and began to remove a layer of rocks so she could look over the edge. One day, while basking in the noonday sun, she saw a traveling woodsman passing by who reminded her of her friends from the journey. He stopped to ask her about her garden, noting some flowers he had never seen before. He expressed his fascination, stating he had never encountered anything so exquisite and wanted to learn more.

She told him to come back the next day and that she would share more about them. For many days, he returned, and they would walk through her garden, discussing all the wonderful and unique plants and flowers that grew there. The scent was intoxicating to him.

The more time they spent together, the more she discovered that he was no ordinary woodsman; he was indeed a prince and protector of small creatures. She did not know that a prince could be kind, gentle, strong, and love gardens as much as she did. The prince lived in his kingdom, a day's journey away, and he invited her to visit. It was earthy, magical, and full of small creatures that he cared for.

Soon, he asked her to marry him, and she said yes. They combined their gardens and created an even more beautiful place to live and be. To this day, they adventure together, tend the garden, smell the flowers, and bask in the noonday sun.

And they both CHOSE to live happily ever after.

The End

# References & Resources

Acknowledgments

Arielle Ford
https://www.arielleford.com/

Clair Zammit
https://femininepower.com/

Jaki Sabourin
https://www.engagedatanyage.com/

Ayanna Mojica
IG: @AyannaMojica
FB: @AyannaMojica

Section One: Preparing Yourself for Love

*The Book of Runes*
Ralph Blum
https://www.amazon.com/book-runes-Ralph-Blum/
dp/0312090013

Arielle Ford
https://www.arielleford.com/

*Move Your Stuff Change Your Life: How to use Feng Shui to get Love, Money, Respect and Happiness* by Karen Rauch Carter
https://karenrauchcarter.com/

*Love Yourself Like Your Life Depends On It* by Kamal Ravikant
https://kamal.blog/book/

Section Two: Healing Your Love Wounds

Alison Armstrong
*Understanding Men* and *Understanding Women* transformational online series
https://www.alisonarmstrong.com/

Serenity Prayer
https://en.wikipedia.org/wiki/Serenity_Prayer

Ho'Oponopono Prayer
https://en.wikipedia.org/wiki/Ho%CA%BBoponopono

Brave Thinking Institute
https://www.bravethinkinginstitute.com/

Agape International Spiritual Center
https://agapelive.com/

A Course in Miracles
https://acim.org/

Michael Bernard Beckwith
https://www.michaelbeckwith.com

Sex and Love Addicts Anonymous
https://slaafws.org/

SECTION SEVEN: WRITE YOUR NEW STORY

Section Three: Preparing For Him

Jaki Sabourin
https://www.youtube.com/@EngagedAtAnyAge

Health Benefits of Gratitude
https://www.uclahealth.org/news/article/health-benefits-gratitude

Gratitude Enhances Health, Brings Happiness—and May Even Lengthen Lives
https://www.health.harvard.edu/blog/gratitude-enhances-health-brings-happiness-and-may-even-lengthen-lives-202409113071
.

Miten and Deva Premal, *Songs for the Inner Lover- Sat Patim*
https://www.youtube.com/watch?v=Fw0UprX9MD8

Section Four: Crafting Your Vision

Wayne Dwyer
https://www.drwaynedyer.com/

Section Five: Pilgrimage, Prayer, and Spanish Rice

Camino De Santiago
https://americanpilgrims.org/history-of-the-camino/

Marianne Williamson, *Enchanted Love; The Mystical Power of Intimate Relationships*
https://marianne.com/books/

Section Six: Getting to the Church on Time

Alison Armstrong - *Understanding Men* and *Understanding Women* transformational online series https://www.alisonarmstrong.com/

Mama Gena
https://mamagenas.com/

Jessica Zweig
https://jessicazweig.com/

Osho Tarot
https://www.osho.com/mobile/zen-tarot

Danielle LaPorte
https://daniellelaporte.com/

Gay Hendrick
https://hendricks.com/?v=5435c69ed3bc

Section Seven: Write Your New Story

Junie Swadron, *Re-Write Your Life: A Transformational Guide to Writing and Healing the Stories of Our Lives*
https://junieswadron.com/

Thank You for Endorsements:

Ayanna Mojica
IG: @AyannaMojica
FB: @AyannaMojica

Cynthia Ambriz
https://www.cynthiaambriz.org/

Lin Yuan-Su
https://enlightenedsuccess.com/

Suzanne Adams
https://suzanneadamsinc.com/

# A Note About Quotes

You may have noticed that I included many quotes throughout the book. Initially, this book was intended as a thirty-day inspirational practice but evolved into a memoir and guide.

I love including quotes and enjoyed searching for just the right one to fit each section I was introducing. Some I had heard before, while others were entirely new to me. I did my best to make sure I credited the correct authors for their quotes. Although I cannot name all the sources I used to find them, *Goodreads* often appeared in my internet searches. I hope that many of the quotes resonate with you and continue to inspire, opening your mind and heart to the most extraordinary possibilities.

# About the Author

Maria Mugica has explored the mysteries of life for over four decades. Born and raised on the south side of Chicago, she departed her hometown with two suitcases and one thousand dollars to seek her fortune in Southern California. There, she found a more expansive life and the freedom to be herself.

At fifty-two, Maria was a first-time bride. She and her husband, Eric, celebrated not just one but three weddings in five months in three different cities. A year later, they enjoyed an extended honeymoon adventure through Portugal and northern Spain.

Maria's greatest joy is helping others transform their lives by overcoming limiting beliefs and creating the life of their dreams.

With the publication of *Happily Ever After is a Choice*, Maria is creating opportunities virtually and in person to go deeper with the practices in this book.

She invites you to get in touch with her via email at maria.mugica@ yahoo.com. Or follow her on Instagram @mariamugica99

www.ingramcontent.com/pod-product-compliance
Lightning Source LLC
Chambersburg PA
CBHW060900280326
41934CB00007B/1125